PETALS FROM THE TREE OF LIFE

(NANA'S BOOK OF WISDOM)

Alison Chant

Petals From The Tree Of Life

(Nana's Book Of Wisdom)

Alison Chant

Copyright © 2023 by Alison Chant

ISBN 978-1-61529-205-9

Published by Vision Publishing
PO Box 1680
Ramona, CA 92065
760 789-4700
www.booksbyvision.org

All rights in this book are reserved worldwide. No part of this book may be reproduced in any manner whatsoever without written permission of the author except brief quotations embodied in critical articles or reviews.

Scripture quotations taken from
The Holy Bible New International Version* NIV*
Copyright 1973, 1984, 2011 by Biblica, Inc.
Used by Permission. All rights reserved worldwide.
Unless otherwise noted.

BOOKS BY ALISON CHANT

UNSUNG HEROINES – AUTHOR AND EDITOR

WALKING IN THE SPIRIT

DIVINE HEALING – THE WONDER AND THE MYSTERY

CAMEOS OF CHRIST

LIFE OF BALANCE -NUGGETS FOR A SUCCESSFUL WALK WITH GOD

MEANDERINGS OF A MEDITATIVE MIND

HISTORY OF VISION

FAMILY FOUNDATIONS

MY MOTHER'S STORY

BENJAMIN – A CHILDREN'S BOOK

God, make me brave for life: oh, braver than this.
Let me straighten after pain, as a tree straightens after the rain,
Shining and lovely again.
God, make me brave for life; much braver than this.
As the blown grass lifts, let me rise
From sorrow with quiet eyes,
Knowing Thy way is wise.
God, make me brave, life brings
Such blinding things.
Help me to keep my sight;
Help me to see aright
That out of dark comes light.

(Author unknown)

Table of Contents

Foreword 7
Introduction 9
Chapter One: Memories 11
Chapter Two: Education 25
Chapter Three: Culture 35
Chapter Four: Building Character 45
Chapter Five: Bringing Up Children 55
Chapter Six: Understanding Your Children 63
Chapter Seven: Obedience 79
Chapter Eight: Encouragement 89
Chapter Nine: Relationships 97
Chapter Ten: The Healthy Family 105
Chapter Eleven: The Dysfunctional Family 119
Chapter Twelve: Building A Successful Family. 127
Chapter Thirteen: Conclusions 135
Chapter Fourteen: Wisdom From History 141
Chapter Fifteen: More Wisdom From History 149
Addendum One 165
Bibliography 167
Words Of Interest 169
People Of Interest 173

6

FOREWORD

It is clear today that many are struggling as the world moves further and further away from biblical mandates on how to raise godly families, build successful marriages and develop positive family relationships. The result is the many tragic stories that we hear about almost daily.

Alison Chant has written this delightful new book that looks at precious gems she has learned and discovered through her experiences as a mother, wife, and church leader.

Alison is already a much-loved author and cofounder of a worldwide ministry. Much of her work has been done while raising a family of five children, including the son she and Ken tragically lost as a newborn. So, to say that she has learned a thing or two about raising children and being a family maker would be an understatement.

Alison did not start writing until she was in her 60s. She has since written numerous books covering subjects such as what it is like to be married to a pastor, marriage and family, walking in the Spirit and living with Christ. Each book is practical and based on her years of experience and knowledge of the Word of God.

"Petals from the Tree of Life" is different to Alison's previous works. In it she shares many jewels of wisdom, all personal to her but with inspiring and encouraging explanations and served up in a format ready to be heard by the next generations.

This is more than just another parenting or relationship book. It is refreshingly different and will encourage, delight, and empower young and old parents, husbands and wives. Alison shows her willingness to invest in those younger than her, which is mandated in Titus 2:3-5 where it says older women are to disciple those who are younger, teaching them how to grow not just in themselves but in their roles as mothers, wives, husbands, and fathers.

Doctor Pastor David Goodwin
International Director and Founder of Kidsreach

INTRODUCTION

This book has been written to illustrate the important questions we should all ask, and the things we should learn to assist us to advance in wisdom and maturity as we grow.

I trust that you, the reader, will gain help from these ideas gained during my lifetime. There is something here for everyone. Things I would like to have known before I began the great journey of life. How to live well and mature into adulthood, find a job, choose a spouse, and start a family.

I believe you will find some help in these pages, if not right now, then on some future day when you need guidance to deal with the great battle of life.

This has been my motivation, to share the information I have gathered over my lifetime. The true to life stories I have added I trust will be of use to you as illustrations of some of the facts in this book. If you learn from the wisdom I have discovered over the years, you will hopefully be saved from some mistakes and indeed gain success and happiness in life.

If so, then you will have a more contented existence and a happier family life. Your children will thank you and be grateful that you have studied to make their everyday experience easier for them in their growing up years.

I must thank Dr. DeKoven for his permission to use some of his material in this book. Other sections I have gathered over the years or learned myself through education. Life itself also offers training and we all gain further insight as we age.

As I have been a Christian since the age of twelve, which was some 76 years ago, this book will have a Christian foundation. For those of you who have not yet made the important decision to accept Jesus Christ as your Saviour I pray this book will help you in some way to make that choice.

Alison Chant

CHAPTER ONE: MEMORIES

The grand essentials to happiness in this life are something to do, something to love, and something to hope for.
(Joseph Addison)[1]

EARLY CHILDHOOD

I was born in 1934 while the Great Depression was still vivid in the minds of the people of Australia, but the poverty and hardship suffered by many hardly registered with me as I grew into a toddler. I can remember a free and unfettered childhood, running around bare foot in the Australian bush in a little settlement named Wangary which consisted of about thirty homes, a Methodist church with its graveyard and a Community Hall. I was the fourth of five children so had older siblings to watch over me.

After teaching us safety rules our mother let us run from dawn to dark, only having to appear for meals when we were hungry or when she blew her postman's whistle to call us in. She had been a kindergarten teacher before her marriage so had many good ideas to keep us happy and well adjusted.

I had countless adventures and never felt deprived even though we had no theatre, no television, no iPad, no computer and not even a corner shop!

Weekends

We played games and searched through the bush for discoveries in nature that we shared with our mother. Our father was away working

---

[1] Joseph Addison (1 May 1672 – 17 June 1719) was an English essayist, poet, playwright and politician.

on his fishing boat in Kelledie Bay each week and we only saw him on weekends. He would arrive home with groceries for the coming week, and a peppermint stick for each of us. He had owned a bakery before the depression but unfortunately this was burned down, and he lost everything in the fire. There were no jobs because of the lingering effects of the Great Depression so he went into partnership with a friend to buy a fishing ketch, and fish for a living.

Nothing was wasted.

I do remember everything was precious and nothing was wasted. We had a huge ball of string which we added to each time we found a new piece. We also had a ball of silver paper gleaned from chocolate wrappings. We saved everything we could because so many things were unavailable in stores. Even our vegetable peelings were used, boiled up and mixed with bran and pollard and fed to the chickens who laid enough eggs to keep us supplied each day.

Now so much is wasted in our society. I'm sure should another depression hit then these saving habits would return. [2]

In my fifth year our family moved to Adelaide. Our father joined the Australian Army of the Second World War and our whole life changed. Dad was away for six years of conflict, but mother was always there for us, a steady and stable influence in our lives as we grew up. I learned much of my wisdom from her.

---

[2] *Currently (2023) about 40% of the total food supply in Australia ends up in the rubbish tip.*

APHORISMS

There were many aphorisms that peppered my mother's speech when appropriate and she learned them from her mother, my grandmother, who learned them from her mother, my great grandmother, and so on through the generations. My husband Ken and I made an interesting discovery in the 1980's while visiting Scotland, the land of my forebears, as we heard the people there still using these same aphorisms which have come down to us through our five generations of Australian settlement.

More than a proverb

An aphorism is more than a proverb, it is a precise statement of a principle. It is a moment of wisdom encapsulated in a pithy saying. My mother reminded us of one or other of these clever sayings at appropriate moments in our family life.

Here are a few of them with suitable interpretations.

A rolling stone gathers no moss.

Those who keep moving house from place to place or change their employment frequently can't accumulate riches. Advancement usually goes to those who are consistent. They are more likely to gather wealth.

A man is known by the company he keeps.

Make sure your friends are people of good character as they will influence you.

A job worth doing is worth doing well.

If you complete the task, you have been given to the best of your ability you are more likely to be given advancement.

A soft answer turns away anger.

These days this is true unless the angry person is on drugs or mentally ill, then it is best to retreat to a safe place.

A man's home is his castle.

We should be safe within our own home but nowadays this may not be true with domestic violence, and the invasion of our privacy with cameras tracking our movements and artificial intelligence monitoring our activities.

A new broom sweeps clean.

This refers to a new boss who tends to get rid of incompetent staff and clear the way for more profits. It could be true of anyone taking on a new job.

Finders, keepers, losers, weepers.

If you leave money lying around your house, then the family member cleaning up should be able to keep it. Don't be careless with money.

One year of seeding seven years weeding.

If you let the weeds grow until they seed, then it will take you much strenuous labour to rid your garden of those weeds.

Take care of the pennies (cents) and the pounds (dollars) will take care of themselves.

Save your cents and your savings will grow. Now with inflation it is the dollars we should be watching.

Sewn with a hot needle and a burning thread.

If a garment is made with cheap goods, it will fall apart.

Never give your name as surety for another person's debt.

You may be left to pay the bill.

My sister, Barbara and I have been remembering yet more proverbs over the last few weeks and here are a few of them.

Ignorance is bliss.

You can't make a silk purse out of a sow's ear.

Listeners never hear any good of themselves.

It was the last straw that broke the camel's back.

Never a borrower or a lender be.

Man is an omnibus in which all his ancestors ride.

Familiarity breeds contempt.

Silence is golden.

Waste not want not.

No doubt there a many more of these proverbs from around the world, but these are the ones my sister and I have never forgotten, and we have reminded each other of them even as I have been writing this book. Their wisdom has stood us in good stead, and we have passed them on to our children and now to our grandchildren.

BIBLE PROVERBS

The book of Proverbs gives yet more solid wisdom on which to build a life. There are many cautions in this book to keep us from making wrong decisions. It contains warnings against laziness, adultery, pride, wickedness, spendthrift habits, bribery, gambling, drunkenness and much more.

As a foundation for life Proverbs tells us that to fear God is the very beginning of wisdom and we are told those who don't respect God or stand in awe of him are fools. We are advised to trust God with all our heart, instead of relying on our own knowledge and wisdom.

Reading this book will assist you to gain insight and understanding. It will teach you sensible and wise behaviour and you will learn to be just and fair in your dealings with others. Even those who are young and uneducated can learn knowledge and discretion and receive guidance and understanding through the parables of Solomon.

Evangelist Billy Graham claimed to read a chapter of Proverbs and a Psalm each day to absorb the knowledge written there. If you also follow this habit, you will learn prudence and have good insight toward living successfully. King Solomon was given wisdom by God as a special gift, and he relayed his observations through his wise sayings. You will do well if you heed the admonitions of Proverbs.

Here are a few of them:

Pride goes before destruction, a haughty spirit before a fall (16:18).

Gracious words are a honeycomb, sweet to the soul and healing to the bones (16:24).

A cheerful heart is good medicine, but a crushed spirit dries up the bones (17:22).

The rich rule over the poor, and the borrower is slave to the lender (22:7).

As iron sharpens iron, so one person sharpens another (27:17).

There are many more proverbs and reading and studying them will cultivate wisdom and may save you from some mistakes in life.

LIFE SKILLS ARE IMPORTANT

Life skills are practical everyday wisdom everyone should be taught by the time they reach their teenage years. My mother taught me the ones I have listed here, and they have helped me throughout my life.

Tact and courtesy

She taught me to be careful to avoid hurting other people's feelings. To think carefully before speaking, and when someone asked for my opinion to try to be honest without being hurtful.

Honesty

When I began working and learning to budget my wages, I was allowed to borrow from my mother if I needed to, but she kept a little notebook, and I had to pay back every penny. This certainly helped me not to get into debt later in life.

Banking

During the war years we had a bank book we took to school once a week. There must have been an arrangement with a local bank for this, and because of it we learned how to save and watch our money grow with added interest payments. Even though we were comparatively poor mother always managed to give us a little money to take to school on Bank Day.

Tax return

This was easy when I first began working but became more complicated over time. We absorb so much by watching our parents and I learned much from observing my parents do their tax returns.

Housekeeping

Mother was an excellent housekeeper, managing on very little during the six years our father was away during the Second World War. She continued to manage on his return by careful spending, and by preserving our fruits and vegetables. She kept an account book and entered the cost of everything she had to buy and so kept track of her spending. This was important as she had only a small allowance and five children to feed and clothe. I learned much from watching her efforts.

She was quite proud of her accomplishments, with good reason. I tried conserving fruit for my family for a season, but with the invention of tinned goods and frozen vegetables our generation has been spoiled. In fact, there is such a variety of preserved foods available that many have lost sight of the fact that home cooking is better for your health.

Rules for boyfriends

Nothing below the neck and nothing above the knees!

Mechanical and home skills

Learning how to look after bikes, motor cars, lawn mowers and power tools. Taking care of a house, changing fuses, replacing seals in dripping taps, repairing cracks in walls, painting and wall papering. These practical skills can be taught by working alongside parents and watching how they do things, or they can be learned through books or practical classes. Nowadays the internet has become most helpful in teaching daily tasks, especially YouTube with its instructive videos on almost everything needed around the home.

These tasks have been traditionally taught to boys in preparation for their future, but girls may also need these skills when they mature, for if a woman remains unmarried or is divorced or becomes a widow, she may need to maintain her own home.

However, skills are not all we need in life as the following quote explains clearly.

> "A person earns their place as a result of three things: Their willingness to practice, their ability to learn from

their mistakes, and their determination to stick with their dream even when success seems out of place."³

If we practice our skills and learn from our mistakes, we can gain a steady work ethic which will help us achieve our goals in life.

However, children should not be promised that they can accomplish anything they want in life, or that they will always realise their objectives. Because their efforts to succeed can only end in disappointment and frustration if they lack the particular skills needed to carry out their ambitions. Attaining success depends a great deal on their level of intelligence, their personality type, their inborn skills, and their determination to overcome obstacles with patience.

> **Life Story.** My husband has often lamented that in several things in which he would love to excel, such as astronomy and classical music. He finally realised he could never become more than competent. He had just enough knowledge to know that he would never be good enough for those two careers. When he became a Christian, his dream was to build a big church for the glory of God, but over the years he realised he did not have the skills to achieve that goal. What he did have was expertise as a writer and teacher, so he changed his dream from building a big church to building a worldwide Bible College instead. In this he succeeded. You can read the story in my book *The History of Vision*.

You can help your children discover their own unique abilities and then assist them in deciding on the education they need. This in turn will prepare them for the kind of job that suits their skill set and will give them satisfaction and happiness in life. Indeed, if you love and enjoy what you are doing your work will not seem laborious at all.

---

[3] Author/Martha Kirkland.

You will appreciate each day and work will never seem to be strenuous or difficult.

Though every child should be encouraged to dream great dreams, they should remain ready to change the dream if things don't work out for them. However, this much I do know, God has a wonderful dream for your life, and he waits for you to discover that dream and to find continuing joy in achieving it.

Family skill sets

Some families have skills that are hands on. They become builders, carpenters, plumbers, brick layers, mine workers and truck drivers. All very necessary, what would we do without them?

Other families use different skills. They become teachers, ministers, soldiers, authors or, because of modern inventions, computer experts. Then a third type of family may become lawyers, doctors, dentists, nurses, counsellors, medical technicians, scientists, architects and the like.

A fourth variety may include athletes gifted in a professional sport, entertainers, artists, dancers, singers, and musicians. A fifth family style could be business minded and enjoy the cut and thrust of industry, and of buying and selling.

If parents can study their own accomplishments and review their family of origin, they should be able to see by their children's teenage years whether they will fit into one of these life tasks. Judging by the interests of the child and by their skill set it should be easy to guide them into the correct avenue of education and preparation. Your children will be wise if they listen to your advice for if they go in the wrong direction here it could take years to remedy any false step.

Although these days with so many new and exciting jobs on offer some have purposely changed direction halfway through their working life. This could cause some financial loss but may also bring more job satisfaction.

My own extended family has produced soldiers, teachers, Christian ministers, authors, and computer experts, though not every single descendent keeps to the family type. Everyone needs to be free to follow their own unique giftings, whatever they might be. At least one of our grandsons has an artistic temperament and paints beautiful country scenes and his sister is fascinated by acting and directing plays and is presently doing a teaching degree in English Literature. Another is in the helping profession and is ministering to the elderly, an expansion of the ministry gifting.

OUR GENES ARE CRUCIAL

Recently I came across an amusing description of the contents of our bodies during a trip to visit my sister in Adelaide. She introduced me to the latest book by Professor Ian Plimer, *Green Murder*, in which he points out at great length the errors of the Greens Parliamentary Party in reference to climate change.[4] I found an amusing and quotable description of our bodies in the book.

> "Some ninety percent of the cells in humans are bacteria and fifteen percent of human body weight is bacteria. You are a creeping colony of critters. Bacteria keep you alive and if one type of bacteria wins the constant biological warfare inside your body then you shuffle off."[5]

We are indeed, fearfully and wonderfully made by the hand of God and originally, he arranged for our body to have the ability to heal itself. If we live right and eat properly then we should be healthy and keep well.

Someone has humorously stated that the only way to be sure of excellent health is to choose your own parents! This, of course being an impossibility, we must inevitably accept the genetic material passed down to us from our parents. If we are blessed, we will

---

[4] I don't necessarily agree with all Dr. Plimer's criticisms which must remain his own.
[5] *Green Murder* by Ian Plimer Connor Court Publishing Pty. Ltd. 2021, pp. 112.

receive a good set of genes enabling us to live a long and healthy life. If on the other hand, we inherit a recessive gene then we will have some deficiency in our makeup which may keep us from perfect wellbeing.

An important concern

Written in the form of a dream:

In this dream Satan was discussing with his minions how to get rid of as many humans as possible before they could hear the good news of the gospel, and various suggestions were brought forward.

> One said, "War and sectarian violence is good as this disgusts people and turns them away from religion. I was hopeful that the atomic bomb would have destroyed humanity, but unfortunately this was a bridge too far and humans drew back from destroying their planet. After all, where would they go if they destroyed this one?"
>
> Another said, "Child abuse is another thing that will turn people away from religion. We have worked hard to tempt certain ones in authority to abuse their privilege and they have become sexual bullies and destroyed innocent lives. This has been going on for a long time. We have a special place in hell for such."
>
> Yet another growled. "The ME generation has done a lot of good work for us! Humans are becoming more and more selfish as they proliferate. Soon there will be so many of them the planet will expire without us needing to assist".
>
> "And there are many in the third world suffering from starvation and lack of pure drinking water", barked another. "We need not be concerned for them for they will die soon enough."

Satan mused, "All this is good, but to attack the Western world we need a subtle approach to trick people into committing slow suicide by self-indulgence.

"And this is what we will do. We will place into the minds of certain ones in our power to pollute the life-giving water on planet earth by creating more potent wines, and soft drinks full of chemicals, especially sugar. Even those who reject sugar drinks and instead drink diet drinks will then be attacked by sugar substitutes, such as aspartame, which are just as deadly.

"Also, we will cause cheap fast foods to be invented which will taste delicious but will bring disease and death to the human race because of the amount of salt, sugar and preservatives in them."

"If we can pervert their appetites, we will win the war!"

"But what if they work out that these indulgences are killing them?" piped up a young devil.

"It will be enough" Satan snarled, "Perhaps some few will escape, but the great majority will continue on ingesting poisons until they die."[6]

Rules for dining

Coming from a very different point of view we have warnings not to over-indulge with food. These come from an obscure 14th century cleric, William Langland.[7]

> "Ah! I know what is wrong with you, said Hunger; "You've been eating too much – no wonder you are in such agonies. If you want to get better, follow these instructions: never drink on an empty stomach, and

---

[6] With apologies to C. S. Lewis and his book *Screwtape Letters*.
[7] *Piers the Ploughman* by William Langland; Published by Penguin Books Ltd. Hammondsworth, Middlesex, England, reprinted 1975.

> never eat until hunger pinches you and sends you some of his sharp sauce to whet your appetite. And don't sit too long over dinner and spoil your supper; always get up before you have eaten your fill. What is more, never allow Sir Surfeit at your table – don't trust him, he's a great gourmand and his guts are always crying out for more dishes."

If you follow his advice, Langland claims you will no longer need a doctor. In fact, your doctor will have to find another way to earn his living for you will be bursting with health. In fact, he had little time for the doctors of the 14th Century.

> "For these doctors are mostly murderers, God help them! – their medicines kill thousands before their time."

Fortunately for us doctors have learned many things in the centuries since and they are still learning. We are told in the book of Daniel that in the last days knowledge shall increase and this includes medical knowledge. Indeed, as I write, because of computers knowledge is doubling every twelve hours[8].

---

[8] http://www.industrytap.com/knowledge-doubling- every- 12- months- soon- to- be- every- 12- hours/3950).

CHAPTER TWO: EDUCATION

Every man is the builder of a temple, called his body...We are all sculptors and painters, and our material is our own flesh and blood and bones. Any nobleness begins at once to refine a man's features, any meanness or sensuality to imbrute them. (Henry David Thoreau)[9]

THE IMPORTANCE OF HEALTH

The lesson you need to heed is this. Be alert, and as much as possible take charge of your own health.

> "We are exposed to toxins in various ways: in the air we breathe, in the water we drink, the clothes we wear, and the food we eat. In our modern world we are exposed to these environmental toxins all day every day. Toxins in our environment can impose an undue external burden on us, while poor digestion, lack of exercise and negative thoughts and emotions can increase our toxic loads internally."[10]

In view of this knowledge, eat as close to nature as you can. Eat meat that has not been covered with preservative, or at least make sure to wash it well before cooking. Also buy fruit and vegetables in season and wash them carefully to get rid of the sprays that the grower uses to kill fruit fly and other insects. As much as possible decrease your use of fast food and carbonated drinks. This earth is polluted enough without us adding to the poisons by eating and drinking unhealthy products. However, I realise we can only do our best and trust God for the rest!

---

[9] Henry David Thoreau was an American naturalist, essayist, poet, and philosopher.
[10] *Never Be Sick Again* by Raymond Francis M Sc. with Kester Cotton; pp. 58-59

Sometimes it is impossible to eat well. Take fish for instance. If it is from the ocean, it can be tainted with the poisons that have been dumped into the sea for generations. If it is from a fish farm, then it is better but still not perfect as this is an artificial way to breed and grow fish. Somehow these fish don't taste the same as the fish I ate as a child, freshly caught by my father.

The true taste of fruit

I feel sorry for the present generation of city dwellers, many of whom don't know the joy of tasting fruit straight from a tree.

Not knowing what it should taste like some people accept the small, unripe, sour specimens that are foisted on them by growers who are trying to get their fruit to market before it spoils.

Fruit only receives the sweetness it should have in the last days of ripening. It is far better to eat fruit and vegetables when they are in season in your area.

Find a market gardener or an orchardist and buy from them and you will be healthier.

> "Commercial practices used to supply food from farms to supermarkets are overwhelmingly destructive. Produce is often harvested before it is ripe, stored for long periods of time and subjected to harmful methods to colour it artificially for presentation in the "fresh" produce section of the supermarket. Some of this produce has lost nearly all of certain vitamins and minerals by the time it rolls down the supermarket checkout lines let alone by the time we eat it."[11]

---

[11] Ibid. pp. 87.

THE IMPORTANCE OF EXERCISE

Exercise is important too. Even if you only walk on three days per week for half an hour each day it can make a big difference to your life. You will be more alert and healthier. You will be less inclined to put on too much weight. Unfortunately, no one told me these things until I turned seventy and then I was advised not to bother because if I did exercise at that age, it would only mean ten more months of life in the Retirement Home. It was not until it was too late that I learned that exercise also increases your quality of life. Be warned, take note and you will be healthier in your old age than I who have suffered knee replacements!

Write your way to good health

Here is another way to a healthy mind and body found in a local paper!

The article maintains that this method literally heals your heart, blood pressure and other stress related diseases. The health benefits of expressive writing have now been scientifically analysed. The conclusions are surprising; while the results show mixed benefits to emotional health, improvements to physical well-being are so big they could be regarded as a major medical advance.

The immune system improves significantly, there were fewer visits to the doctor, improved lung function, improved liver function, and fewer days in hospital. It even seems to improve available memory.

After three writing sessions lasting twenty minutes on consecutive days; some months later people suffering asthma, recorded better lung function, and those with rheumatoid arthritis had less inflammation and pain.

The mind and body are more connected than we think!

Here are the writing instructions

Write about your deepest feelings for twenty minutes every day for the next four days.

Write about the most traumatic experience of your life or an emotional issue that has affected you.

Really let go and explore your deepest emotions.

You might tie your topic to your relationships with others, including parents, friends and lovers, and to your life, past, present and future.

You can write about who you have been, who you would like to be and who you are now.

You can write about the same issue in each session, or about different topics each day.

What you write is entirely confidential, not to be seen by anyone else. Once you start writing continue until the twenty minutes are up.[12]

Writing in this way will reveal your emotions, some may grow angry as old hurts are revealed. Others may grow tearful as they write for the same reason, but the results are very liberating and can indeed help you to a healthier mind and body.

THE IMPORTANCE OF EDUCATION

When I was young and wanted to go to Teacher's College my parents could not afford the fees. Instead, I had to go out and get a job to support myself. So, when I became a young housewife and

---

[12] If you are interested in more study on this subject, then you can find it in *The Body Keeps the Score* by Bessel Van Der Kolk under the heading, *Writing to Yourself* pp. 284-289.

mother, I decided to educate myself. I did this by joining the local library and reading as many classics as I could.

It is good also to read biographies of great men and women. I enjoyed the biographies of remarkable Christians such as Mary Slessor, and David Livingstone. In the last chapters of this book, I share some of the famous people from whom I have learned interesting insights.

Good books for young people

In my youth my mother introduced me to *Pilgrim's Progress* by John Bunyan and *Little Women* by Louisa May Alcott; Nature books such as *Freckles*, *The Girl of the Limberlost*, *Laddie*, *The Keeper of the Bees* and *The Harvester* by Gene Stratton-Porter; *Anne of Green Gables* and all the Anne books by L. M. Montgomery, and many other good wholesome books suitable for a young girl.

Nowadays I shudder at the dark depressing books that are offered to young people. Surely it is better to give every child suitable literature to read that will teach them good morals. This will help to improve their character and so increase the possibility of them living a happy and successful life.

I challenge you to take up at least some of the books I have recollected and see if you can enjoy them as I did.

A balanced education

I read many books to my children, and they all became book worms as they grew old enough to read for themselves. This is a great way to educate your children and teach them to read at an early age.

The Narnia Series and other books for adults by C. S. Lewis are a must for a balanced education. *Mere Christianity, The Screwtape Letters, The Great Divorce, and Surprised by Joy* are all worth reading, especially for anyone interested in Christianity and searching for truth.

Those of you that enjoy science fiction would enjoy Lewis' Science Fiction books. Even though they may seem old fashioned now with all the latest technology, we still hold a profound message.

My husband and I both enjoy the hilarious books by the English author P. G. Wodehouse, and we often get a talking book of his from the local library, to listen to on one of our long car trips. Wodehouse is not to everyone's taste, but we enjoy him.

My husband, Ken would want to add adventure books suitable for young boys, and he would include theology books, poetry, and classics such as Shakespeare's Plays to my list. It would take a lifetime to experience all there is on offer. Reading good, knowledgeable books teaches and educates a person in many ways.

Modern literature for children

The suggestions I have made may seem very old fashioned to modern youth who have been taught from books such as *Lord of the Flies* by William Golding and have read the *Harry Potter* books by J. K. Rowling, and the collective volume of the thirteen books of *A Series of Unfortunate Events* by Daniel Handle. These have all been made into movies. These books, and other modern books for children, I find somewhat dark, and depressing compared to the books that were available to my generation.

The Anne books, *Little Women, Pride and Prejudice*, some of Dickens and many others of the older generation have also been filmed but these remain an outline of the full story, so it is always more satisfying to read the book that inspired the film.

Unfortunately, with television, iPads, personal phones and Kindle, reading real books with the pleasure of holding them in your hand and turning the pages has become less popular. However, if the internet should ever go down permanently through a catastrophic event, then books will come into their own again.

Some best sellers

There is a plethora of new and exciting authors today but the one I am most interested in as I write is Eric Metaxas. He has a conservative radio program, also a popular interview session he calls *Socrates in the City* whereby he invites important thinkers to be interviewed in front of an audience. These conversations can be found on You tube.

He is a prolific author and has written several biographies which have been best sellers.

Bonhoeffer, - Pastor, martyr, prophet, spy.

Martin Luther – The man who rediscovered God and changed the world.

Amazing Grace - The story of William Wilberforce who ended slavery in Britain.

Also, an autobiography of his own called *A Fish Out of Water* explaining his search for truth and his ultimate discovery of Jesus Christ and salvation, which I enjoyed immensely.

Eric Metaxas has written another book, *Is Atheism Dead?* He wrote this in answer to the question, *Is God* Dead? put forward by Time Magazine in 1966. In the first section of his book, he indicates that science, with its exciting discoveries of the fine-tuned universe makes belief in a creator more certain. In the second section he covers archaeological discoveries that have proved the Bible is an accurate history. In the third section he mentions the many scientists who are Christians and refutes other atheistic scientists with their arguments against belief in the God of the Bible. This is an important book for Christians as it gives answers to questions asked by people who have received a modern education including Darwin's theory of evolution. [13]

There is another important aid to mental health beside reading good books and that is overcoming loneliness through friendships.

THE IMPORTANCE OF FRIENDSHIP

Loneliness is a crippling condition that can cause much unhappiness, so it is good for us to have friends we can love sincerely. What kind of love should we have for our friends? There are three kinds of love, and each come from the heart and arise spontaneously. They are romantic love, family love, and brotherly love, and it is brotherly love we usually feel for our close friends who are dear to us.

There is yet another kind of love, and this is the kind of love God has for us all. He treats us, both saint and sinner, alike because he is a God of justice. His kind of love shows his good will. He wants the very best outcome for our life.

We can also show this kind of God-like love by deciding to love others as God does. Then, even if we don't like certain people, we can still love them by showing good will toward them and wanting what is best for them.

This decision to love as God loves should also result in compassion for the person living on the street and for the beggars of this world because a homeless person is not always to be blamed for their situation. A crippling illness can bankrupt an individual and leave them destitute through no fault of their own. So, with God's help we can love the unlovely, but there is yet another important point about friendship.

---

[13] if you would like to go more deeply into these ideas try dr. Stephen Meyer's book *The Return of the God Hypothesis*.

Friendship can be lost

Friends who have good will for one another, and who agree together on everything, and have a shared purpose, can still lose their closeness to one another if they rarely see each other. For instance, if a friend moves interstate or leaves the church or club that you formerly attended together then you can drift apart over time unless you make a strong effort to keep in touch.

Dale Carnegie on friendship[14]

When you are talking to someone, Dale Carnegie suggests you show an interest in their life and opinions and meanwhile look cheerful and smile a lot, because no one is attracted to a person who looks miserable and is always complaining.

Carnegie also insists you should listen carefully to what the other person is saying, making comments that show your interest, and then encourage the individual to talk about themselves. Last of all, he suggests you learn how to make the person feel important and mean it sincerely.

Do you find it hard to make friends? Extroverts have little trouble attracting friends, but if you are an introvert and find it difficult, try to make the effort to appear warm and friendly. You will be surprised how this will encourage others to try harder to develop a friendship with you.

Slowly but surely, you will find many interesting companions who will enrich your life with true friendship.

> "A real friend is one who, when you've made a fool of yourself, doesn't feel you've done a permanent job."[15]

---

[14] *How to Win Friends and Influence People*, by Dale Carnegie.
[15] https://quotes.yourdictionary.com/author/erwin-t-randall/564542

CHAPTER THREE: CULTURE

One of the most important phases of maturing is that of growth from self-centring to an understanding relationship to others…a person is not mature until he has both an ability and a willingness to see himself as one among others and to do unto those others as he would have them do to him. (H. A. Overstreet)[16]

GOOD MANNERS

It is the common belief that it is money or love that makes the world go round. I'd like to submit that it is not only these two but also good manners that keeps life progressing acceptably.

Years ago, I read of a club in England that taught good manners. It claimed to have saved many marriages! Yet another club wouldn't allow swearing on their premises. Anyone who swore had to pay a cash penalty because the members considered profanity to be bad manners.

Along with lack of communication and financial stress, bad manners can be at the root of many divorces.

Translated simply, the proverb, "Manners maketh man" means that politeness, good manners, and civility are essential to humanity.[17]

I always taught my children to look people in the eye and shake hands firmly on a first meeting. We were polite to our children, and they learned to be polite from our example.

---

[16] Harry Allen Overstreet (1875 – 1970) was an American writer and lecturer, and a popular author on modern psychology and sociology.
[17] This proverb is believed to have derived from the century's old works of William Horman (c. 1440 – 1535). He was a headmaster at Eton and Winchester College in the early Tudor period of English history.

The rules of good manners

Two hundred years ago, a gentleman always walked on the roadside of the footpath to protect his lady friend from any danger. This was because his sword was worn on his right hip, and he needed his right hand free to draw his sword if danger threatened. In the 20th Century a polite gentleman would also walk on the right, but it would be to protect his lady companion from any dangerous traffic.

Gentlemen also opened doors for ladies, though nowadays with electronic doors sometimes this politeness is unnecessary. They also spoke gently to them, and never ever lifted a hand against them!

How different it is these days, some women in their fight to be like men, refuse the opened door and want to fight back verbally, if not physically, when quarrelling with their husband or partner. A consequence of this kind of arguing with some couples can result in domestic violence and sadly one woman dies from this brutality almost every week here in Australia.

Where politeness and mutual respect are part of the innate philosophy of life guiding a couple, neither husband nor wife will be violent toward each other, either verbally or physically. Rather, they will discuss every issue great and small with love, respect, patience and kindness.

Tact is very important

As mentioned in chapter one tact is one of the rules of good manners, we all need to learn tact.

> "Tact is a keen sense of what to do or say in order to maintain good relations with others or to avoid offence."[18]

In other words, be careful not to embarrass another person by what you say to them. And never speak derogatorily to them in front of

---

[18] Webster's dictionary.

others. If you have anything to say that is at all negative at least wait until you are alone with the person, or they will not accept what you have to say.

Return to the Golden Rule

Do to others as you would have them do to you. If you want people to treat you with tact and consideration, then you should deal with them in the same way. Be careful in your speech, if you can't say anything pleasant or positive then it is usually best not to say anything at all.

Elegant speech

Good manners surely will also exclude anything that may be offensive to others, such as blasphemy and swearing. It is good to remember the biblical adage not to swear by the heavens or by the earth. If we are wise, we will learn good manners, with both tact and elegant speech so we do not offend others. Pleasant speech offends no one, but crude speech offends many.

The Bible definition of great wisdom is that it is first pure, then peace-loving, considerate, submissive, full of mercy and good fruit, impartial, and sincere. If we follow this definition in our conversation, we will never carelessly upset another person by our speech.[19]

Manners within the family

We only had a few rules for our children related to good manners. Be obedient, and don't lie, don't bully, don't swear and don't be rude or "give cheek". Now I realise how negative this was. It would have been far more positive to teach the encouraging aspects of family life such as good manners, cooperation, good speech, obedience, and truthfulness.

---

[19] James 3:17

WOMEN'S LIBERATION

Women's liberation has changed our culture and some women today, because of birth control, demand the same freedoms men have always claimed. Freedom to have one-night stands with sexually transmitted diseases as a result. Liberty to swear, get drunk and fight with each other. Abandoning good sense and good taste to wear as little as possible, leaving nothing to the imagination. Some freedom!

It is hard for a decent man to find a good woman and vice versa. No wonder couples are having to find each other on a computer program. Of course, they could try joining a church youth group. That is where my husband and I found each other. My Christian girlfriends all found their life partner in the same church and as far as I can ascertain all those marriages stood the test of time.

This year Ken and I will celebrate our 69th wedding anniversary. We have had a very happy marriage and there are many reasons for this contentment.

CHOOSING YOUR LIFE PARTNER

When Ken and I met and were attracted to each other we asked many questions. We learned we came from a similar background and social standing. We discovered we had one parent from each family a teacher, both our fathers enjoyed football, and they both voted for a labour Government. We were both Christians, we both loved children, we agreed on how to discipline children, and we both wanted to go into full time ministry. There was only one year difference in our ages, Ken being one year older than I. With so many similarities in our family background we knew we were constructing a firm foundation for our marriage.

Look and listen

I liked the fact that little children and domestic animals all seemed to be drawn to Ken. I thought he would make a good husband and father. One thing I had been taught was important. *"Listen to the way your boyfriend talks to his parents as that is the way he will talk to you after twelve months of marriage"*. Similarly, the man should listen to the way his girlfriend talks to her parents for the same reason.

Life Story: One married couple I counselled many years ago had a serious problem. He had been a submariner and was obsessively tidy bordering on OCD (Obsessive, compulsive disorder). He had colour coordinated shirts and coat hangers in his wardrobe and it was irritating for him to live with his wife who was a happy go lucky type. She had no idea how to run a home. She was always in a mess, and this did not bother her at all. I could see no easy solution for this couple, unless they loved each other extremely well and learned to tolerate each other, they would not be able to make a happy family life for their children.

Life Story: Another scenario I have seen more than once is the combination of a melancholy husband with a sanguine wife. Initially the melancholy is attracted to the sanguine because they are so bright, sparkling and effervescent. But unfortunately, after a few years of marriage the sanguine wife becomes subdued and miserable, unable to withstand the constant negativity of her husband. Or perhaps the effervescent wife after a time irritates and annoys her sombre husband. If I had the opportunity, I would not advise either of these types of couples to marry.

BLENDING TOGETHER

We became firm friends during our courting days and learned tolerance and patience from each other. I just knew we would have a successful marriage as all the possible differences had been talked through and eliminated before we became engaged. This has proved correct with scarcely any differences of opinion over the many years of our living together in marriage and raising our children successfully.

It is not essential for the general uniformity we enjoyed for a couple to construct a happy marriage, but it certainly helps in getting along well as you understand each other perfectly. If a couple do not have this mutuality of background, they can still have a happy marriage, but they will have to work harder to understand and appreciate one another.

Waiting for marriage

We found it hard to wait for marriage as we were going together for nine months and then engaged for another nine months. Fortunately for our desire to remain chaste, we were separated for many months of our engagement. Ken was 500 miles away studying for Christian ministry in Melbourne, Victoria and I was living with my parents in Adelaide, South Australia. One good thing about this was that we continued to learn about one another by writing to each other frequently and I had many long letters from Ken as he was and still is, a prolific writer.

Common law relationships

Presently, young people live together before they marry, and sometimes they do not bother to marry at all. If you are a Christian couple, then surely you need to ask God's blessing on your coming together by going through a marriage ceremony. Although Isaac only had to take Rebecca into his tent to satisfy the requirements of marriage in Bible days, the Jewish people soon set up a ceremony for joining two young persons in marriage. In the following centuries contractual arrangements were made between families to join their children in wedlock and these were sanctioned by the church.

Later in Britain, because of the increase of nonconformist preachers who were not bound by laws already in place, a House of Commons

Committee recommended the setting up of a National System of Registration and the introduction of civil marriage as we know it today. This took place on 1st July 1837.

Here in Australia young people can either marry in a registry office or make their vows in a church setting. There are marriage celebrants also who will conduct marriages in any setting chosen by the couple who wish to marry.

I would be happier were my grandchildren to be traditional and stay with a marriage covenant celebrated in a church rather than just living together with their partner. So far, I am pleased they are preferring a marriage contract.

If young people rush into a sexual relationship without making any vows to each other first, they will miss the joy of getting to know one another gradually and experiencing all the thrill of young love. The result is they may have a superficial relationship which cannot help but falter when life gets difficult as life always will!

Don't cheat your future spouse

Young people who have sexual relations with many partners before they marry will have less of themselves to give to their marriage. Each time they give part of themselves away in a sexual relationship they are cheating their future marriage partner. They will not come to their wedding ceremony complete and unsullied. This will count against a lifetime commitment, making it harder to avoid divorce if differences arise.

THE PROBLEM WITH HUMANISM

There is a Christian joke concerning humanism.

> "Some people believe in many 'gods', some believe in one God. The humanist, however, believes he is God."

This is true of many humanists though not all, some are acknowledging that there must be a God. Even Sir David

Attenborough, English broadcaster, writer and naturalist has been known to say, "Actually there probably is a God."

In 2012 Alain de Botton, wrote a book "A Religion for Atheists." He claimed that Christians, because of their beliefs, have better mental health than those who are atheists. He cited many Christian habits, such as meditation, forgiveness, and community as being good for your physical and mental health.

Losing respect for authority

I do not know how anyone can be so foolish as to believe everything on this earth of ours just evolved from nothing, without a designer. Humanists who do not believe in a god, or indeed in any type of spiritual existence, have caused harm in a social sense because when people stop believing in God, they lose their respect for authority, both God's ultimate authority, and the earthly authorities God has ordained for the good of mankind.

Having no belief in the spiritual world reminds me of the biblical Sadducees. They didn't believe in angels or heaven and that is why we Christians joked they were so "sad-you-see". Are Humanists the modern-day Sadducees? Certainly, they share a disbelief in the unseen spiritual realm though humanism goes further into philosophy.

What does the humanist believe according to Wikipedia?

> "**Humanism** is a democratic and ethical life stance, which affirms that human beings have the right and responsibility to give meaning and shape to their own lives. It stands for the building of a more humane society through an ethic based on human and other natural values in the spirit of reason and free inquiry through human capabilities. It is not theistic, and it does not accept supernatural views of reality.

Infiltration Into schools

Humanism has infiltrated our universities and many of our lawyers, judges, and teachers have spread the philosophy far and wide. In my opinion this humanism has much to answer for. The breakdown in the family and the social fabric that comes from an atheistic lifestyle has weakened our nation.

Humanists may refute this but if so then what other explanation can they bring forward for the present-day mental illness caused in part through the ME -generation. For instance, in the USA today there are six million children on psycho-tropic drugs for ADHD and Bi-Polar disorder.[20] This is a catastrophe waiting to unfold as these juvenile brains, that are still developing, are bathed in chemicals to control their conduct. I am concerned to think what the future holds for these children and in consequence for the nation of USA. Our own nation of Australia is using chemicals to control children with difficulties as well. Only time will prove how much damage this is causing.

Be informed

What can we do about these things? We need to become educated on what is happening in this country and in the wider world, and study what can be done to turn things around. We can also reveal to others that there is a God of love who created all things and who cares about ordinary people and their problems. A God of love who will help them if they can put their trust in him.

The spiritual realm

Young people these days are reaching out to the spiritual realm. They are turning away from materialism which has not brought them

---

[20] Clinicians call ADHD a neuro developmental disorder, meaning that it affects a person's behaviour, memory, motor skills, or ability to learn. Bipolar disorder is persistent changes in mood, characterised by periods of either very elevated moods (hypomania or mania) or very low moods.

the happiness they were promised. One result is there are thousands of university students who have become Christians, and this could be the beginning of a change in our culture.

If you are a Christian, then you must be always ready to give an account of your faith to anyone who inquires why you believe as you do, though good manners will wait for the question to be asked!

It is a good idea to pray each day for opportunities to speak to those who are ready to listen. Always be prepared to give an answer to everyone who asks you to give the reason for the hope of salvation that you have. But do this with gentleness and respect. [21]

---

[21] 1 Peter 3:15

CHAPTER FOUR: BUILDING CHARACTER

I hope I shall always possess firmness and virtue enough to maintain what I consider the most enviable of all titles, the character of an "honest man". (George Washington)[22]

CHARACTER FORMATION

"Character is the product of daily hourly actions, words and thoughts, daily forgiveness, unselfishness, kindness, sympathies, charities, sacrifices for the good of others, struggles against temptations, submissiveness under trial. It is these, like the blending colours in a picture, or the blending notes in music, which constitutes the man or woman."[23]

Those words of John Rose Macduff deserve contemplation as they give a good description of what it takes to build a good strong character which can influence others. Indeed, going without can be good for your character.

Life Story: The year I turned seven years of age I discovered that Father Christmas was my Mum and Dad, so I determined to stay awake until my presents were placed by my bed. When they tiptoed in, I thought I heard them mention a pink coat. I was so excited as my sister, Barbara, and I had no new clothes, but only handed down dresses from our cousin, Fay because of the poverty of the war years. My sister wore the dresses first and then when it came to my turn the clothes were

---

[22] George Washington (1732 – 1799) was an American military officer, statesman, and Founding Father who served as the first president of the United States.

[23] https://quotes.yourdictionary.com/author/john-rose-macduff/78915

third hand and somewhat worn. To have something new was wonderful, and of course for it to be pink and not some dull serviceable colour was a bonus.

My dreams were shattered next morning when I discovered I had misheard my parents and was now the possessor of a brown school case, not a pink coat! A tragedy for seven years of age, but now that I am in my eighties it seems trivial.

Disappointments make us stronger

But disappointments do make us stronger! We who suffered deprivation during the Second World War years grew up robust, able to handle the frustrations of life. We learned to look ahead to a brighter future. After all, we were taught the British way, stiff upper lip, and forge ahead regardless!

Looking around today and seeing so many giving up on life with no courage or future potential I thank God for my deprived childhood. Going without a few material possessions was a small price to pay for a character able to withstand future shocks.

At Christmas times we should pause to think of the millions who are not just deprived of toys but of food and water, the very necessities of life. They are robbed even of any hope for the future. How blessed we are in this land of Australia. We should thank God for his blessings every day, that we have enough and to spare for others.

WHAT FATHERS FACE TODAY

In *Making Your Children's Ministries Count for Eternity* Daron Pratt says,

> "Modern affluent societies overflow with a range of goods produced for the entertainment, pleasure, convenience and education of our children."[24]

Then Sharon Beder in *This Little Kiddy Went to Market* has this to say:

> "The consequences of the corporate capture of childhood have been a generation of children who have been manipulated, shaped and exploited like never before in history...Not only have they lost the opportunity to play and develop at their own pace, but their psyches have been damaged, and their view of the world distorted. Children have never been under such pressure to succeed, conform and look good. The result is that now we have adults sitting in the psychologist's office saying, 'I don't understand, I had wonderful parents, they gave me everything and yet I feel empty inside and I am unhappy.'"

The age of materialism and humanism has not filled the life of the average person with happiness, and they are now articulating their unhappiness. They are hungry instead for the spiritual aspect of life.

What do fathers need to know to help them in their parenting in this modern age?

Some characteristics belong to God alone

He is Sovereign, He is all Wise, He is all Powerful, He Knows all Things, and He Is Everywhere Present. This is stated unequivocally in the Bible.

> *Nothing in all creation is hidden from God's sight. Everything is uncovered and laid bare before the eyes of him to whom we must give account* (Hebrews 4:13).

---

[24] From an unpublished set of notes *Celebrate Children*, edited by David Goodwin from Kidsreach Missions 2011.

No ordinary father has these godlike qualities and so cannot be expected to be a perfect father. Most strive to do the best they can, and we cannot expect more from them.

WHAT GOD SAYS ABOUT HIMSELF

When God began to reveal himself to the patriarch Moses, he showed the characteristics of a loving father.

> *The Lord, the Lord, the compassionate and gracious God, slow to anger, abounding in love and faithfulness* (Exodus 34:6).

These characteristics of not being quick tempered, of having compassion, love and faithfulness are possible for our earthly fathers to emulate with God's help.

And there are many other wonderful things about God for fathers to copy in their dealings with their children. For he is also affectionate and just, generous and accepting, he communicates, and he disciplines.[25]

PAUL'S WISDOM

> *For you know that we dealt with each of you, as a father deals with his own children, encouraging, comforting, and urging (exhorting) you to lead lives worthy of God, who calls you into his kingdom and glory* (1 Thessalonians 2:11-12).

These same three things, **encouragement, comfort, and exhortation** are also to be the basis of a pastor giving an encouraging word to an individual in a church setting. In other words, we adults need the same reassurances that children require.[26]

To encourage means to give courage, to give confidence, to inspire.

---

[25] See Addendum One for Scriptures.
[26] 1 Corinthians 14:3

After love, trust and necessary discipline, encouragement is the most important gift to give your children. On the other hand, discouragement will hamper your child throughout life, causing depression and fear to haunt him or her as they mature.

How can you discourage your child?

You can discourage your child by expecting too much of them at their stage of development or by not giving adequate instruction before demanding obedience from them.

How to prevent discouragement

It is natural for children to want to obey and please their parents but if this is not the case the reason is discouragement.

When you train a little child, they go on what they feel or on what has been demonstrated to them. You cannot teach them; you must show them what you want them to do. So, training involves showing them how to do things such as have a bath, tidy your toys, and take out the rubbish bins.

Teaching can start at about the age of eight years, and you can begin by explaining why you want them to do a particular task, and then how to accomplish it. As they grow older, they can be taught other more appropriate chores. Children need to be trained to become fully functioning adults.

To Comfort means to give solace to a person.

There is something about the love and comfort a father gives his children they can receive from no other source.

A father's love is different

> "A mother's love is lovely and irreplaceable, but there is something about a father's love which to an infant imparts a sense of strength, of security, of being important, of being valuable. If a child does not get that

love of his father, then he will have a deep inner wound. A sense of being unimportant or unwanted."[27]

If there is no father in a family through death or divorce then a father figure, such as an uncle, should be encouraged to be a role model to help the child mature. This is important for both boys and girls as they both need a father figure someone they can look up to as an example of fatherhood.

To urge or exhort means to use words of argument to arouse or spur on to good deeds. The exhorter is always looking forward and seeks to inspire to good works, such as helping those in need.

The effect of separation or divorce

If a father leaves his child through separation or divorce, then that child will always feel inadequate. He or she will carry a wound throughout their life.

Divorce leaves a deep wound, especially in the young and vulnerable but also in those who are older. Even though they may overcome their sense of loss and have a successful life the pain never really goes away.

> **Life Story.** Two brothers, James, and Harold, suffered greatly from their parent's divorce. After their parents separated, they were constantly let down by their father who would promise to take them on holiday. They would pack their bags and be waiting with excitement for the treat, but then their father would not turn up. They were left with no explanation. This happened time after time until they finally realised their father had abandoned them for good. Their mother remarried and their stepfather tried to do his best for them but without much success. The older boy managed to overcome his disappointments as his character was already formed before the divorce. However, his younger brother never

---

[27] https:www.Derek Prince.com.au

recovered from his father's rejection and grew up to become involved with drugs and ended up with a prison sentence.

Fathers have a great responsibility

Fathers, your children cannot see God, but if you are kind and loving they will believe that God is kind and loving. If you are just and consistent in your discipline yet forgiving and kind when your children are sorry for doing wrong, then they will see God as just and forgiving.

PARENTS NEED TO GET A GRIP.[28]

Dr. Michael Carr Gregg of Melbourne Children's Hospital says,

> "Children need a charismatic adult, someone who makes them feel safe and who consistently sets boundaries... (But) there has been a melt down with Australian parents in the past few years. I've never seen it so bad... (The result is) an unprecedented level of depression and anxiety among children."

Communication is very important to children. However, Dr Gregg goes on to say,

> "Don't lecture or have too many deep and meaningful conversations... Not too much eye contact, talk about things while doing a task together, such as washing the dishes... do fun things together...But don't try to be best friends with your teenager, give them boundaries and

---

[28] The Information from Dr. Gregg and Dr. Bennt came from *The Sydney Sun Herald,* Thursday 11th December 2003, and August 26th 2004.

they will feel secure. Fathers, your ultimate goal is to produce an adult who is decent and self-reliant."

Then Dr. Bennet of the Children's Ward of Westmead Hospital advises,

"Across all social groupings the kind of parenting that works is authoritative; warm, nurturing and responsive; firm and demanding of maturity; fostering and encouraging psychological autonomy."

PARENTING TYPES

They can be authoritarian and rigid, threatening to punish the child for any disobedience! Or passive, letting the children rule, thus setting themselves up for chaos!

Then there are the latest parenting types. Tiger Mums and Helicopter Parenting.

Tiger Mums try too hard to fill their child's life, with soccer, music, ballet and other extra-curricular activities, not giving them time to play, or to just be children.

Helicopter parents hover over their children, watching everything they do, making sure they perform well.

The lesson for fathers today is this:

Don't make the mistakes that others are making. Father your children as God has instructed you in the Bible, encouraging them, comforting them, and exhorting them to mature into responsible adults!

Be a good father. Set a fine example to others, love God and love your children. Encourage them, be firm and consistent in your discipline and teach them to make right choices for their own ultimate good.

Life story. One of my earlier memories of my father gives me pleasure. He had been away for six years during the Second World War. He left when I was five and returned when I was eleven, fighting first in Tobruk and then in New Guinea. On this day our family were all together holidaying on the Murray River, Northeast of Adelaide. My father woke me early one morning and took me down to the river to fish. He caught some fish and then cooked them for our breakfast over an open fire. That fish tasted delicious, but what meant more to me was the fact that my father had taken time to spend with me, just the two of us. There were five children in our family and there is no doubt in my mind that our father did something like this with each of his children, seeking to restore his loving influence over us.

CHAPTER FIVE: BRINGING UP CHILDREN

The ideal which the wife and mother makes for herself, the manner in which she understands duty and life, contain the fate of the community. Her faith becomes the star of the conjugal ship, and her love the animating principal that fashions the future of all belonging to her. Woman is the salvation or destruction of the family. She carries its destinies in the folds of her mantle. (Henri F. Amiel)[29]

WISDOM FOR MOTHERS

"Mummy gives chocolate and presents, and she cuddles me when I'm hurt. She gives lots of love and helps me when I'm sad." (My grandson Sebastian 5 1/2 years of age).

What do mothers face today?

The great gods of money, affluence, degenerate television films, drugs, trans-genderism, trans-humanism, the ME generation and more!

How can she raise her children with God's help?

Mother love should not be sentimental, it must be strong and determined, yet deep and consistent. My own mother showed this kind of love. She was strict but loving and kind. She was frugal and hard working. She worked hard to give us a good childhood with plenty of time to play. After she finished raising her children she worked as Honorary Secretary to the Local Government Women's Association. She was clever and earned a Queen's Jubilee Medal and an Order of Australia because of her untiring work over many years. I honour her memory.

---

[29] Henri Frédéric Amiel (1821-1881) was a Swiss moral philosopher, poet, and critic.

Mothers should cultivate the fruit of the Holy Spirit to assist them in their mothering. This translation is from the Message Bible.

> *"What happens when we live God's way? He brings gifts into our lives, much the same way fruit appears in an orchard – things like affection for others, exuberance about life, serenity. We develop a willingness to stick with things, a sense of compassion in the heart, and a conviction that a basic holiness permeates things and people. We find ourselves involved in loyal commitments, not needing to force our way in life, able to direct our energies wisely"* (Galatians 5:22-23).

Some things a mother can do

She can be authoritative (fair and consistent) but not authoritarian (rigid and unbending). She can teach her children the Ten Commandments in simplified language suitable for them.

Character and self-esteem will be formed in children by the time they are ten years of age, and if they are not taught God's rules for living by then they will lie and steal without any sense of shame.

Forming character

A mother can help to form good character in her children by providing books that depict people who show honesty, integrity, and kindness to others. By reading these books together and then discussing the excellent qualities portrayed she can hopefully foster good solid character traits in the life of her children.

It is good sense to remember that the battle between nature and nurture is a definite problem for parents. Especially for those who take in foster children. The ratio used to be thought 50% nurture and 50% nature but sadly it is more 25% nurture and 75% nature. Some believe that no matter how much you teach children to be good, honest, and well mannered, nature will always win over nurture.

Life story: Two foster girls, Margaret and Raelene, were brought up lovingly by a pastor and his wife and were progressing well until they reached around 14 years of age. That year the Department of Child Welfare insisted each one should meet their birth father. From that moment they told the pastor who had helped raise them that he wasn't their real father, so they didn't have to obey him anymore. They proceeded to go quite wild for a few years getting into drugs and sleeping around causing much sorrow to the pastor and his wife. Ten years later they have pulled their lives together and have settled down to marriage and motherhood. For them, as for many other foster children, nature took over from nurture. The genes have a very strong influence over a person's life no matter how well they are loved and cared for in a family situation. In this case Christian virtue finally triumphed.

Life Story: Amazingly, it does not always follow that the child will follow their gene pool. Two boys with an alcoholic father had different outcomes to their life. One grew up to become an alcoholic like his father but the other one grew up to stay sober and diligent and built a good life for himself. When asked why they finished as they did both men said the same thing. *"What else could I do with a father like mine."* One decided to give way to his father's weakness, the other decided to avoid his father's weakness.

THINGS TO AVOID

Don't be a tiger mum who is ambitious for her child and who will persuade, push, and control her child to gain success in school. Or a helicopter parent who hovers over her children watching everything that happens, trying to keep them safe and successful. Both these types of parenting can become quite aggressive and may express belligerence towards the teacher of their child if they think it will help the young person to achieve top marks.

On the other hand, don't be a permissive parent either, allowing the children to rule, or chaos will be the result.

Instead, try for balanced parenting and an environment that is both relaxed and invigorating with time for both play and study.

Remember, children need plenty of hours to imagine, to dream and to enjoy their playtimes because this is essential for their brain development.

How does God mould the Christian?

As a young Christian, when we first begin to trust God, he gives us many easy answers to prayer, but then he expects us to begin to make our own decisions based on what we have learned from the Bible. In this way we grow into maturity in Christ.

Following God's example, we should gradually allow our children to begin to make their own decisions after we have taught them the guidelines.

One simple instance is to let them choose their clothes for the day. If they choose clothing that is inappropriate, that is clothing that makes them too cold or too hot, then they will learn better next time.

Find out what interests them and encourage them to follow their ambitions, whatever they may be. Children should be free to follow their own path, finances permitting, and not be locked into fulfilling their parent's desires.

A quote from a teenager

> "Mothers can be fun, and I know mine loves me, but sometimes she is too controlling, and she always want to know everything I do." (Carol 16 years)

Gradually and carefully letting go of a teenager can be a difficult time for parents, but we must let them grow, develop, and make a few mistakes. If we are there supporting them with our love and concern, they should not go far wrong.

Christian mothers are blessed

Even though mothers have difficulties in our present culture in bringing up their children, they should count their blessings. Think of those mothers in the third world who have little education and for whom it is a daily struggle to house and feed their children. We should indeed be grateful we were born in this land of Australia.

Teach your children what they need to know

If you are a mother, pray and trust God to help you with your children. Speak blessing into their lives, raising their self-esteem so they will gain the strength and maturity to live a good life, with a bright future.

There are several kinds of love as mentioned in chapter two. There is romantic love for a spouse, family love for members of your family and brotherly love for a friend.

There is also a godly love which desires a good and happy life for everyone. God's love indicates he desires the best and most useful life for us with opportunities to succeed in our chosen field, so we should seek his advice for our important life decisions. If we do, then we will make fewer errors and achieve more satisfaction as we mature.

Above all mothers should love their children

> *"Love never gives up, Love cares more for others than for self, Love doesn't want what it doesn't have, Doesn't have a swelled head, Doesn't force itself on others, Isn't always 'me first', Doesn't fly off the handle, Doesn't keep score of the sins of others, Doesn't revel when others grovel, Takes pleasure in the flowering of truth,*

Puts up with anything, Trusts God always, Always looks for the best, Never Looks back, but keeps going to the end." (1 Corinthians 13:4-7 Message Bible).

PARENTING THE CHILDREN

There are three types of parents.

Authoritarian - Strict and rigid in command, they demand blind obedience.

Libertarian – Those who hardly discipline at all. In contrast to their own parents and their rigid discipline some parents now are too permissive. They don't set proper guidelines or boundaries and the children feel insecure. They give too much to their children and children who are given everything they want don't appreciate anything! Worst of all, if only material things are given without love, then children will become angry and miserable.

Egalitarian – This is more balanced than the first two, those who determine to parent fairly are strict, when necessary, but also wise and able to think ahead and avoid confrontation. They use consequences rather than physical punishment as soon as the child is old enough, usually seven to ten years. These parents deal with grace and forgiveness. They know how to reward cooperation, acknowledge feelings, set limits, teach skills, communicate love, and model self-esteem. They devote lots of time to their children. During the teenage years these parents learn to negotiate. Some things are set in stone, but others are negotiable. This teaches the teenager how to make decisions and what is fair and equitable for the whole family.

Modern pressures

Parents today are under unique difficulties, torn apart by family and work responsibilities. Filled with guilt they hesitate to discipline their children. They tend to buy them things to compensate for not spending time with them.

But children who always get what they want straight away do not develop any resilience, strength or toughness for living. They tend to collapse when life gets difficult, especially in their teenage years. It is far better for them to go without or to have to wait for what they want for a time. This way they learn valuable lessons, that life isn't always easy and that we can't always have everything we want.

Then there are further tensions from television news, worries from school, peer pressure from friends and an uncertain future with chaotic world events transpiring.

What the Bible has to say

The Bible has a lot to say about rearing children. The plan is to talk about God and his precepts, and rules for successful living, as often as possible bringing the concept of God into the life of the family. Along with loving God with all our heart we are to teach the commandments to our children and then talk about them continually as we go out and about. All day long, from morning to evening until they know them by heart.[30]

THERE ARE NO GUARANTEES

However, even if a person were a perfect parent, as God is, still there is self-will to cope with. God has many rebellious children.

There are no guarantees that we will succeed with our children, but we need to learn as much as possible to do a good job of raising them. This is even more necessary today. Because of the nuclear family, with relations scattered and distant from one another and so many divorces, the wisdom from the grandparents has not been handed down as it used to be.

---

[30] Deuteronomy 6:5-7

Now there are many who do not know how to be a wife, a husband, or a mother or father. They have had no role model from which to learn.

We do learn some things from our family of origin without realising it. We are trained by what we see and hear throughout our growing up years. When it is time for us to parent, we automatically either follow our parent's style or we rebel against it by going the other way, determining instead to be different in the bringing up of our children. Many parents are on automatic pilot. They just assume they will know what to do because of what they have observed in their own family.

In conclusion, parenting should be based on what is good for the child and on the instruction given in the word of God. If these guidelines are followed it will go a long way toward rearing a child who will be a blessing and not a curse.

CHAPTER SIX: UNDERSTANDING YOUR CHILDREN

The domestic affections are the principal source of human happiness and well-being. The mutual loves of husband and wife, of parents and children, of brothers and sisters, are not only the chief sources of happiness, but the chief springs of action, and the chief safeguards from evil. (Charles W. Eliot)[31]

BEGIN WITH LOVE

Newborn babies begin to either feel safe and to trust or, if they are neglected, to feel insecure. Babies must learn to trust, first their mother and then their father. If they are adopted, then they must learn trust from their adoptive parents.

If a baby has its bodily needs met, that is feeding and changing, but does not have its emotional needs met, that is being hugged and talked to, it will not develop as it should.

Recently a man noted that the babies in the orphanage he was visiting were very quiet and did not cry at all. He asked the reason and was told the babies used to cry when they first arrived, but the nurses were too busy to answer them, so they gave up. How sad for those little ones who will not grow and develop as they should. It is vitally important for babies to be picked up and cuddled regularly for they may die young if their emotional needs are not met.[32]

Children this age also need continuity and consistency. They have an attention span of three to five seconds. Continual positive reinforcement of smiles and hugs will cause babies to increase their response and they will begin to react positively.

---

[31] Charles William Eliot (1834 – 1926) was an American academic who was president of Harvard University from 1869 to 1909.
[32] https://aifs.gov.au/cfca/publications/understanding-child-neglect.

Parents must create an environment of safety and nurturing for their baby. If instead they are inconsistent, punish, or abandon their little one at this age they will only teach the child mistrust, that they are bad. This is all they can understand. Trust is essential for the spiritual, emotional, and physical development of the child.

CARING FOR FOSTER CHILDREN

> *"Understanding foster care is like learning about a foreign country. If you are not from there you don't speak the language. Life is upside down for foster care youth. The security and love other children take for granted they have to create for themselves."*[33]

Children have a limited chance of learning trust if they are taken from their birth parent, and especially if given more than one placement by the age of eighteen. Life is bewildering for them as they travel from one family to another, often with different sets of rules to be learned in each home. It must be tormenting for a child to be shouted at for something they were commended for at their last placement. No wonder so few of them succeed in life.

> **Life Story**. One problem in going from home to home is that there is a difference in the parenting skills of the people involved. Peter was a dear little boy, aged six years and he loved to sing; he would sing himself to sleep at night and was contented and good. As he was only in a temporary situation the time came for him to go to a permanent placement. Within a few days of this new home, he became unmanageable, very aggressive, so much so that he tried to stab one of the children in his class at school. Everyone was puzzled as to how this change from a calm happy boy to such an aggressive monster could have happened. After asking questions of the temporary parents and the new parents the family doctor discovered that in the temporary home Peter had

---

[33] https://www.pinterest.com>pin

no sugar as that parent was diabetic and did not allow sugar in the house. The new placement parents however had tried to win Peter's affection by buying him many chocolates and other sweets. When the sugar was removed from Peter's diet, he once again became a calm and happy boy.

It is this kind of misunderstanding foster children may have to contend with, it is no wonder they are seldom truly happy. The best life for children is to have parents that love them and treat them well so their family can stay together.

THE IMPORTANCE OF BONDING

As discussed in chapter three, it is important when choosing a spouse to choose someone who has a similar background to yourself.

Choose someone of the same race, if possible, someone on the same social level, who has attended a similar school and has reached a similar level of scholarship. Someone whose family have the same view of politics. If this is done, then as parents the two of you will have many ideas in common.

The relationship between husband and wife should be sacred, a covenant together so that no other person can break that bond. It is essential for the union to be successfully accomplished so the two become one as we are told in Genesis.[34]

It is the man who leaves his parents to cleave to his wife. The woman on the other hand, though she will bond with her husband, still needs to turn to her mother for advice and assistance, especially when she has her first baby.

This is born out by a popular Irish aphorism, but God was the first one to point out this truth in Genesis.

---

[34] Genesis 2:24

> My son is a son till he takes him a wife,
>
> a daughter is a daughter all of her life. [35]

Families should agree

When two people come together they should take time to agree on the raising of their children. They need to work out guidelines for parenting before the children come along. If the parents have come from different backgrounds and different family types, there will inevitably be some things they have to work through.

Some families have short fuses and discuss everything from politics to sex at the top of their voice. Others have very contained families who rarely discuss anything and hide their feelings.

If individuals from these two disparate families marry, then it takes a lot of grace to work things through. One must learn to control their temper and discuss things more quietly; the other must learn to express their feelings more openly yet in a gracious manner.

What must be learned when it comes to rearing children is that consistency and agreement are paramount.

Work things out together

Parenting is an outgrowth of a relationship between husband and wife. No one, adult or child, should come between the marriage bond, or between the relationship the parents have with one another.

For couples to be effective in parenting they must begin with a firm foundation based upon principles they can approve. They must agree also to be faithful to keep their word to one another and so keep a united front before the children. If they do this their children will have boundaries that are consistent and they will feel much more secure, even though they complain and continually test these boundaries!

---

[35] https://www.pinterest.com>pin

Decisions must be made and adhered to because if a child senses a difference of opinion in his parents, he will play on this to get his own way. Children are very clever, and they will divide and conquer if you give them half a chance. They will go from one to the other trying to get their way.

Self-concept – who am I?

By the time children are ten years of age their self-concept is fully formed. By this time, they know who they are, what they are about, their feelings, their importance, their sense of worth or lack thereof. So, the time from birth to ten years is vitally important.

SECURITY

If a child is brought up without a father, they will bear a wound, a lack of self-esteem, for the rest of their life. Unfortunately, these days fathers are many times absent through desertion or divorce and unless this trend reverses there will be an increasing number of boys being brought up by a mother only with deleterious effects.

Mothers are also very important, they give love and compassion, but fathers are equally important, they give a strength to a child, a feeling of security that the child needs desperately.

If you have a child with low self-esteem, it could be rooted in the formative years because either something happened to discourage the child or else, they suffered a lack of security or love.

> **Life story:** My maternal grandmother, Alice, suffered a lack of security from which she never fully recovered. Her parents had a large family, and they were asked, by relatives who were childless, if they could take one of their daughters and give her a better life with more opportunities. The relatives chose Alice who was then six years of age. It is not hard to imagine what an effect this had on this little girl, taken from her large family of loving parents and siblings, and taken to live as an only

child by a couple who had no real understanding of children and their needs.

My grandmother did receive a better education and was playing the church organ at the age of eleven. However, she never recovered from this separation from her family and still in her 90th year said to me sadly, "*Why did they send me away.*"

I realise that her parents thought they were doing the best they could for Alice, but the situation certainly had a deep effect on her throughout her long life. Her security and the love of a large and boisterous family were taken from her without her being able to understand why it was happening. Instead, she went to loneliness and people who, though they treated her well, did not really understand what she was going through.

Eventually she grew up and married a man chosen for her by her adoptive parents as those were the days when arranged marriages were a normal way of life. She had seven children and my mother, Laurel, was the baby of the family. Alice had a long and industrious life with much to be thankful for, but there was always that question in her heart which robbed her of so much self-esteem.

HOUSE RULES.

As mentioned in chapter three we did our best as parents with some simple rules we established in our home –

No cheekiness. Our children were not permitted to speak back to us.

No bullying. The elder was not allowed to bully the younger.

No swearing. We insisted on clean speech, no matter what they heard outside our home they were not permitted to use those swear words at home.

No disobedience. If our children disobeyed there were consequences.

No lying. This was a tough one as children will lie if they fear punishment. We assured our children if they were honest, and admitted guilt, if indeed they were guilty, they would not be punished but instead receive a lecture on honesty being the best policy.

> **Life story.** There is nothing worse for a child than to be disbelieved when they are accused of doing something of which they are innocent. When I was very young and playing with my siblings in the back paddock of our property our elder brother, James swore. We children had been taught this was not permitted, so we ran home to tell mother what our brother had said. Unfortunately, his legs were longer than ours and he reached our mother first to tell her that we had sworn! Mother believed him and she washed our mouths out with borax. I can still remember the horrible taste of that borax. Parents believed in rough justice in my youth and mother's philosophy was that our mouths needed to be cleansed from the swear words. My siblings and I never forgot this indignity when we were innocent of any wrong. This story became a family saga and we never let our big brother forget his perfidy. We were still reminding him of it in his old age even though he grew up to become a preacher of the gospel!

We supported one another

Once our family rules were decided on my husband and I always supported one another. Ken would never allow the children to disobey me. He would always support me and as the boys grew older and stronger, they were never allowed to use their superior strength against me.

And as I mentioned in chapter three, instead of punishing for the negatives it would have been better to be more positive in our approach and instead praise and reward good manners, cooperation, good speech, obedience, and truthfulness.

We did on occasion apply discipline to the seat of learning, in other words we spanked our children, when necessary. They were born from 1955-1970 when spanking was not frowned upon. We never had to discipline in this way after the age of seven and our grown children later thanked us for the lessons they learned. Because we were never unduly harsh our children seldom resented our discipline which stood them in good stead as they matured.

The ideal family would perhaps use a combination of these positive and negative rules, but each couple must decide for themselves how they will parent their children.

I realise that now in the 21st Century it is frowned upon to spank a child but sometimes nothing else will do. Perhaps there would be much less delinquency now if there had been a little more discipline when the children were small. In my opinion it is quite safe if the parent's hand is used as the parent feels the punishment as well as the child.

As grandparents my husband and I now feel that we were too hard on our children and thinking back we would rather have used different methods to gain obedience from them. Parenting is not easy, and each person must decide for themselves how strict they will be and what methods they will use.

Practise makes perfect and lectures on parenting are very helpful for those who are having difficulty with their children or are unsure of what to do sometimes.

PROBLEMS WITH PRE SCHOOLS

Children suffer sleep deprivation from being aroused early to go to the Nursery, or Pre School and then, unless their teachers give them a rest period after lunch, they lose more sleep.

This constant lack of sleep is bad for their immune system.

Germs spread more easily when children are together, and children do not get the same individual attention they would receive from their parents at home. It is always best for very young children to be at home with their mother where they are safe and well cared for. Just this week in New South Wales a young child died because of carelessness on the part of his minders who were not well enough trained. These accidents can happen and cause intolerable grief for families.

While sleep deprivation, germs, and insufficient training of staff are possibilities to guard against, still some parents must work if there is a desperate need for finance.

Sometimes a single mother or a widow needs to work to support her family. Each person must work out their needs and act accordingly. But it is a good idea to search carefully until you find a Nursery you feel you can trust with your precious child.

Basic training

The ten commandments are basic training. God did not give us these rules to make us miserable but because he knew if we kept them, we would lead a happy productive life.

We knew this so we had them on the wall of our home!

Behind the toilet door is a good place where time for contemplation is enhanced, but make sure you have them written in language suitable for children to understand.

The Good News Bible has an appropriate translation which I have simplified for little ones but as the children grow older the correct version should be used.[36]

---

[36] Exodus 20:3-17

Commandments for the little ones

1. Love God best of all, respect him and be in awe of him. Do not worship any other god.
2. Don't worship things that fly, walk or swim. Worship only God.
3. Don't use God's name, or the name of Jesus, as a swear word or in a joke.
4. Go to church to praise and worship God on Sunday.
5. Honour your parents by obeying them and caring for them in their old age.
6. Don't kill or even bully others, instead be kind and compassionate.
7. Don't love someone you should not love.
8. Don't steal anything from shops or people.
9. Don't lie but always tell the truth.
10. Don't want what belongs to someone else or be jealous of them and what they have. Be content with what you have.

It would be a good idea to discuss these laws with your children and make sure they understand them. God's commands build respect for authority into children, and they will need to have this respect for authority to live a peaceful, joy filled life.

Children will do what you do, not what you say

Children must not only learn the basic statutes of God, but they must also see these worked out in the lives of their parents. It is very important for parents, and indeed all authority figures, to practice what they teach. In other words, they should be consistent in their living standards and not have one requirement at home and another level of behaviour at church or when they are outside the home.

A parent's primary goal is to teach their child to fear and respect the Lord and in turn to respect authority. It is because there is no fear of God that lawlessness prevails in our land and larger and larger prisons are being built.

Include your children

Children should be included. Jesus' disciples thought children were a nuisance, but this was not how Jesus felt and he rebuked his disciples for trying to exclude them. Jesus' treatment of children was loving and kind, he blessed them and used them as an illustration of the innocence and humility we all need to enter the kingdom of heaven.

So, children should be included in the family circle when visitors are present. This teaches them appropriate ways to behave in company. It is good for their self-esteem to be included as much as possible.

It is loving, appropriate touch which affirms and builds value and self-esteem in children. Only parents can provide this, for in the present climate here in Australia, with so much abuse of children in the press, it is forbidden for teachers to give a hug or even a pat on the back.

But when children are fighting then teachers are allowed to break up fights. Horrifying footage was shown of a Sydney School fight, with one boy left lying motionless on the ground after being hit on the head.[37]

The Education Code (2014) recognizes that teachers (and other certificated employees) have a responsibility to intervene physically in order to protect students. A teacher may use reasonable force in order to quell a disturbance, protect others, in self-defense or to take possession of weapons.

---

[37] https://www.triplem.com.au

CHURCH GOING

It is good to bring your children to church and teach them appropriate behaviour, because it is better for families to worship together if possible. However, long meetings that are not easy for children to follow should be avoided. Sunday School is the appropriate answer for children to learn the Bible stories and the lessons gained from them depending on their age level.

THE DESTRUCTION OF THE FAMILY

Slowly but surely the family unit is being destroyed by our modern culture. The selfishness of the ME generation and the slow decline of the authority of the church are part of the reason for this. Also, the inevitable result of a vast advertising conglomerate tempting people to buy more than they need. Because of this both husband and wife have to work to manage the expenses of a family. In consequence their children are left to be minded by others for long hours each day.

What is the present status of women?

Jesus raised the status of women to a high level during his earthly ministry. A woman, Mary, was chosen to be his earthly mother and another woman, Mary Magdalene, was the first person given the wonderful news of his resurrection. The Apostle Paul continued this trend in his writings and urged men to love their wives sacrificially as Christ loved the church.[38]

Throughout history in western countries the status of women has fluctuated from time to time. In some eras they have been nothing but chattels with no rights of their own, in other eras they have been emancipated and able to hold important positions and even run a business of their own.

Now in our modern era they are claiming, not only freedom to be whatever they want to be but are also challenging men by proving

---

[38] Ephesians 5:21-23

they can do almost anything a man can do in every sphere of life. They merely lack the physical, muscular strength of the male.

How did the present emancipation of women first begin?

It was partly the invention of all the labour-saving devices that have proliferated since the beginning of the modern era that slowly but surely freed women from the drudgery of the past and made it possible for them to demand a different way of life. If these had not been invented women would still be tied to the home. As it is they have been set free from the hard work of keeping the home clean, cooking meals on cast iron stoves and sewing clothing for the family by hand, which prevailed during the centuries past.

What happened during the 20th century?

> "Beginning in October 1918, the Soviet Union liberalized divorce and abortion laws, decriminalised homosexuality, permitted co-habitation, and ushered in a host of reforms that theoretically made women more equal to men. The new system produced many broken marriages, as well as countless children born out of wedlock."

As of 2021, Russia still has the highest rate of divorce according to United Nations data from 2011. Their divorce rate is 4.8 divorces per 1,000 residents.[39]

In Australia the divorce rate peaked in 1976 at 4.6 per 1,000; it is currently around 2 per 1,000.

In Britain during the Second World War (1939-1945) while the men were away fighting in the trenches women began to take their place in the factories and on the farms.

---

[39] https://worldpopulationreview.com/country-rankings/divorce-rates-by-country.

> "It seems to me that the family unit became disengaged from each other beginning after World War 2. Women began working out of the home. People (were) also working for companies that required their employees to transfer to multiple locations in the country (or internationally) throughout their careers."[40]

Now, with Women's Liberation and women proving themselves capable of many of the tasks previously filled by men, wives are combining keeping a home going and working in a secular job. However, this can be exhausting and cause much dissatisfaction in the family circle even with the modern inventions that help with housekeeping. Also, husbands are beginning to fight back against this trend of working wives because it brings about the destruction of their original function as protector and provider and if divorce does occur it is sometimes difficult for fathers to access time with their children.

> "Nonetheless, women are fighting hard to preserve their newly gained emancipations, and it is unlikely that the conditions, say, of the 1940s will ever be restored. So, we may have to find new ways to strengthen family life. After all, the ideal woman, whose price is far above rubies, was a prosperous businesswoman, and where was her husband? Sitting in the city gates gossiping with his friends. No wonder he proclaimed her priceless, surpassing all other women."[41]

Last of all, there is the homosexual and lesbian movement and the LGBTQI controversy which also mitigates against the traditional family unit. Even though these groups are only a small percentage of the population they have a determined voice on their own behalf. And now that we have entered the era of being able to have surrogates to bear babies, homosexuals can have children. This

---

[40] Commonsensehome.com/destroyed-extended-family/
[41] *My husband Ken Chant's opinion of the present situation*, citing Proverbs 31:13-22.

means there are many different ideas of family life in Australia today.

In contrast the original family unit is very important to God.

God's original idea of family is the best way and the right way. Families with a mother and father and children makes up the strength of a nation. As they honour God and his laws, he will protect them and prosper them. The care for children flows from the heart and purposes of the Lord through the parents, who need to be living in a loving healthy relationship with one another. The stronger the family, the stronger the nation. Today the deterioration of the family unit has made our nation of Australia weaker.

CHAPTER SEVEN: OBEDIENCE

*Be ever soft and pliable like a reed,
not hard and unbending like a cedar (Talmud)*[42]

A BRIEF OVERVIEW

The early years of life are critical for development. A child's main way of learning and developing is through language and play, these are the two most important tools. They learn to play together and share their toys. Other influences on development include the genes they inherit, nutrition, physical activity, health and community, the modern influences of television and iPads and other electronic devices. [43]

MILESTONES

0-1 years -Children's early experiences and relationships teach them to trust their care givers. If they are not loved and talked to and their needs are not met, then they will instead learn mistrust. At this age they also gradually learn to copy actions, such as waving goodbye.

1-2 years -Toddlers learn autonomy, how to exercise their will and do things for themselves. If this is not encouraged, then they will doubt their abilities and feel shame and doubt.

3-5 years -Children learn to initiate tasks and carry out plans. If this is not permitted, they will feel guilty about efforts to be independent.

6-12 years- Children at this age need physical activity to build strength, coordination, and confidence. Communication and interaction with others are important. They can think intelligently about

---

[42] The Talmud is the central text of Rabbinic Judaism and the primary source of Jewish religious law and Jewish theology. PAF 101 Module 3 Lecture 2
[43] From *Psychology* Eighth Edition by David G. Myers, Pub. Macmillan 2006

concrete events. Children learn the pleasure of applying themselves to tasks. If this does not happen, they will feel inferior.

Teenage years are a time of dramatic change for both boys and girls. This is the age at which the body begins to shift from childhood to adult. This is a time of change in how they think, feel, and interact with others. Teenagers work at refining a sense of self by testing roles and then integrating them to form a single identity. If this does not happen successfully, they become confused about who they are. This confusion has reached epidemic proportions in the 21st Century with much agony of mind for both parents and children.

BASIC SKILLS OF CHILDREN

It is right for children to be taught obedience from an early age and disobedience should be punished, but it is not easy for a child to obey inconsistent or unreasonable requests or demands that go beyond their capabilities.

If a parent asks a child to do something that is beyond their evolving skills, then the child will become discouraged.

If a child is not developmentally ready for a certain task and the parent treats this inability as disobedience this is not fair and the child will become bitter, resentful, discouraged, and angry.

Parents need to make it their task to find out the basic skills of children and the ages at which they ought to be able to take on tasks.

A CLOSER LOOK

Age 2 is the age when children learn to say, *"No"*. It is the age of autonomy versus shame and doubt.[44] Autonomy means the freedom to monitor oneself. From 18 months they begin to explore their environment, to climb, and jump. They must be observed constantly at this time without being too restricted.

---

[44] Op Cit *Parenting On Purpose.*

House proofing

At this age the child desires to control everything in their environment. They think they own everything, and they want to touch everything. They have no conscious sense of guilt and must be taught morals and behaviour by the parents.

The parent's responsibility here is to child proof the home so it is safe for the child to explore. This is the time for setting boundaries and limits. The child must learn what is allowed and what is expected. Boundaries must be set to develop self-control in the child. At this age the child wants to control everything!

POTTY TRAINING TIME

This is controlled by muscle, emotion, and psychology.

The reason the child says, "*No*" all the time is because it is easier to say than, "*Yes*". They will say, "*No*" when they mean, "*Yes*"! Parents should learn this is normal for this age.

Potty training should begin when the child shows interest in learning control. If you start too young it won't work!

One woman boasted to me that she had never had to use a napkin on her baby, but she had to watch her baby constantly and had no time to do anything else.

Another put panties on her little girl at twelve months, she still had accidents for a while, but it was easier when girls wore dresses all the time. Now the fashion is for jeans for both boys and girls, this is not feasible.

Remember you are dealing with issues that go beyond the potty chair. You can be stubborn, but children can be more stubborn. When they are ready it will be easy. Boys can learn by watching Dad or an older brother.

If after they are potty trained, they have an accident because they waited too long by continuing to play and putting off asking for the toilet then there should be consequences such as helping to clean up.

Over control

Rigidly controlling anything, including potty training when taught by the parent can cause shame and self-doubt. The child then feels incompetent; that he/she can only do what the parent says they can do.

Lack of control

In contrast if children are allowed to do whatever they want they get a sense of omnipotence. This is a disaster, but they will eventually discover they are not the centre of the universe and cannot control everyone.

Most children this age want to control others, especially mum and then dad, but you can't give them everything they want, you must be in control.

Parents who are immature and impulsive themselves will become frustrated by a wilful child. They will feel out of control and then the child will try to take command. This must not be, by careful and consistent discipline a child will learn to obey.

Discipline

> Discipline is training that corrects, moulds, or perfects the mental faculties or moral character.[45]

Loving discipline at this stage is for the parent to show by example what is acceptable and what is not. You can gradually eliminate inappropriate behaviour by constantly changing the child's direction and giving them something else to think about.

---

[45] Webster's Dictionary.

Make sure to choose the best times for teaching obedience. When a child is overtired or unwell it is best to postpone the moment. Look ahead and you will save yourself many a struggle.

> **Life Story:** We had a friend whose little boy sought to dominate his parents and control them by holding his breath whenever he was asked to do something he didn't want to do. Our advice was not to be concerned because even if the child turned purple and lost consciousness he would then automatically begin to breathe, and this proved to be the case. Children can be very clever and soon know if what they are doing will stop you from demanding obedience from them.

TEMPER TANTRUMS

> "Do not allow your child to throw tantrums. Freedom that is unrestrained results in a character that is unbearable. But total restriction leads to a servile character."[46]

These wise words from an ancient Roman philosopher prove that children have always had the same problems growing into maturity. There needs to be a balanced approach to discipline.

Children can throw themselves down and roar with rage when they are frustrated at not getting their own way. My husband only allowed each of our children one such tantrum. If he was present any time after that they did not risk another bout of temper. There is something about a scolding from their father that a child responds to quickly. In contrast the mother's voice is either too soft or too familiar to have the same effect.

Unfortunately, because some parents have been cruel and harmed their children, laws have been passed for all parents and teachers,

---

[46] *365 Stoic Quotes* by Lucius Annaeus Seneca who was a Roman philosopher (4BC – 65AD).

making it impossible for them to apply any bodily punishment at all to a child.

Indeed, some parents these days are afraid to spank their child because they are terrified the child will be taken away from them. They feel helpless to discipline in that way and must use other means, such as restrictions to gain control of their child. Other parents do not believe in corporal punishment of any kind and discipline their children by requiring them to remain in the "naughty corner" for a short time while they think about what they have done.

Some believe children who are never spanked could grow up thinking they are boss over their parents, with the sad result that they might possibly be in danger of developing a superiority complex. This in turn could make them selfish individuals who may perhaps destroy much of the happiness of their own future family.

Children prefer strict parents who make them feel safe and secure. A child who is not disciplined is not truly loved.

What does the Bible have to say?

> *No discipline seems pleasant at the time, but painful. Later on, however, it produces a harvest of righteousness and peace for those who have been trained by it (*Hebrews 12:11).

In other words, discipline produces well-behaved children who are a blessing to their parents.

Childish Secrets

When a child of two or three years becomes secretive it is because they are trying to create their own autonomy, that they are a separate person. Wise parents will give them room to grow and develop their separateness.[47]

---

[47] *Journey to Wholeness* by Dr. DeKoven; Vision Publishing 2000

At this age they will not share well, and they may take things without asking. This is normal and will gradually change as they become more aware.

A parent's purpose is to bend the will but not break it. They must also make sure they speak clearly, so that the child knows what is required and understands and is able. If all these things are in place and the child is deliberately disobedient then some punishment, such as consequences is required.

At the ages of **four and five** the child wants to please mum and dad in everything they do, and they are keen to try many new things, perfecting their skills of language and imagination.

When they reach **six to twelve** children begin making things to please their parents. They want to show their parents they think they are wonderful. Parents must be careful at this age for if they criticize their child too much instead of encouraging them the child will develop a feeling of inferiority. They will think they are not good enough to please mum and dad.

Expressing feelings

All parents should teach their children that it is alright to express feelings but that this must be done with respect.

In Ephesians 6:4 the apostle Paul teaches fathers not to exasperate their children, but to bring them up in the training and instruction of the Lord.

Don't provoke anger

Remember! People provoke their children to anger and discourage them when they have either asked them to do something that they are not capable of doing or have set an expectation on them that is too great for them to handle, such as adult behaviour. This creates initial frustration, leading to internalised unresolved anger.

The result of abuse

Children who are sexually abused are children whose natural boundaries have been broken. They do not know how to respond and so internalise its message of rejection and betrayal. They become discouraged, live in denial, and ultimately face a life of depression and despair.

If only sexual predators were aware of the terrible trauma they cause!

> *Jesus said, "If anyone causes one of these little ones - those who believe in me - to stumble, it would be better for them if a large millstone were hung around their neck and they were thrown into the sea" (Mark 9:42).*

THE GOAL OF PARENTING

The goal of all parenting is for the parent to raise a responsible citizen, able to function in relationships and in the work force, with the ability to delay gratification and work toward goals that will be satisfying to them.

Discipline has four components the parent must provide.

Clear expectation, explaining clearly what is required.

Supervision, watching to see the child has understood and is able.

Follow through and

Encouragement. This is very important!

Training for tasks

It is the parent's responsibility to show how things are done until the child knows the routine and then to follow through and make sure the task is done correctly and on time.

Once this is done then the parent can trust the child to do the task without supervision. If the child "forgets" or decides not to do the task on any day, then there must be consequences for this.

Don't be too rigid with time, a grace period is allowable and when a job is well done the child deserves praise.

Don't be armchair parents, check up on jobs

Don't just yell at them as this teaches them procrastination that is delaying or postponing the task.

Good work ethics

Children need to learn to be responsible then they will grow up with a good work ethic, but they will not learn unless they are supervised and held accountable.

CHAPTER EIGHT: ENCOURAGEMENT

Anyone can carry his burden, however hard, until nightfall. Anyone can do his work, however hard, for one day. Anyone can live sweetly, patiently, lovingly, purely, till the sun goes down. And this is what life really means (Robert Louis Stevenson)[48]

POSITIVE SELF ESTEEM

To encourage and inspire is more powerful than to praise and admire. Negative behaviour is produced by negative or damaging words spoken.

Children can remember forever the scathing words of a parent or teacher, such as "You are hopeless, you will never amount to anything."

Positive self-esteem is built by a pat on the back or an affectionate hug and then an encouraging word. This builds up positive affirmation!

Some parents are afraid to say, "*No*" to a child at all in case they bruise their ego or break their will, but this is nonsense. Children need boundaries, it makes them feel secure. Inspiring words go a long way toward producing positive and constructive behaviour.

Puppies are trained by using positive reinforcement. Each time they do something they have been asked to do they get a treat. While our children are far more precious than our pets it still follows that they also respond to positive reinforcement. So, rewards for good behaviour and ignoring bad conduct as far as possible may be the

---

[48] Robert Louis Stevenson (1850 – 1894) was a Scottish novelist, essayist, poet and travel writer. Best known as the author of *Treasure Island* and *The Strange case of Dr. Jekyll and Mr. Hyde*.

way to go. Though, if the misconduct is serious, it will obviously have to be dealt with.

The ME generation

Western Culture teaches materialism and self-centredness. But as Christian parents we need to teach a different culture, one which does not need to accumulate vast possessions, and which puts the needs of others first.

The parent's first task is to teach maturity and the second is to teach the Golden Rule:

> *In everything, do to others what you would have them do to you, for this sums up the Law and the Prophets* (Matthew 7:12).

That is, children should be taught to be polite and kind to other children if they want other children to be polite and kind to them. That will be as much of the golden rule as they can understand at their age.

Parents who are sincerely kind and loving will have the best results in bringing up their children because they themselves have learned to be tolerant and thoughtful. Because of this they will not be cruel to their children but seek to nurture them with patience and firmness.

If you make a mistake

No one is perfect so learn to admit mistakes yourself if needed. This gives your child permission to admit mistakes also.

Learn the grace of forgiveness. A child is very forgiving and needs to know they are forgiven also when they do wrong. Never let unforgiveness go on into a new day. *Do not let the sun go down while you are still angry.* (Ephesians 4:26).

Forgiveness is very important in family life

> "Forgiveness works "like oil" in relationships. It reduces friction and it allows people to get close to each other without overheating. Without "forgiveness" in fact, relationships freeze up like an engine a few quarts short on oil."[49]

CHILDREN ARE INDIVIDUALS

Even though they are alike they are all different and special in their own way.

Children 4 to 6 years of age will begin to show initiative.[50]

This is the time when children want to do things without constant supervision. They are trying to master their environment.

A sense of responsibility begins to assert itself. Small goals are beginning to be achieved. Goals such as going next door to play with a friend by themselves. A moving away from mum and dad but still wanting to please them.

They begin parallel play, swapping toys but not really sharing. However, at this age if they do too many things that are not properly or positively rewarded, they will feel guilt.

The virtue for this age is finding a purpose for living. They are learning to take initiative which makes them feel part of the family system. This is still a pre-learning stage. If they are pushed into school too early, they will feel inadequate.

The latest findings are that children who are fast tracked by their parents with flash cards and other educational material are not any further ahead by the time the end of grade one is reached. Parents may well leave their child to relax and enjoy life, play and allow

---

[49] https://www.josh.org/daily-devo/the oil of relationships.
[50] Op Cit *Parenting on Purpose*.

their brain to develop slowly but surely. The child will do better and feel better for it.

Is your child ready for school?

Don't send your child to school before they are ready. If you do, you will set your child up for guilt and failure which can then be carried for the rest of their life. At five years of age your child could breeze through learning to read words and understand numbers, or they could fail because their brain was not quite ready for these tasks.

If they were not ready to learn this could make school difficult and taxing for them instead of easy and fun. Just one more year at home playing would give their brain time to develop and would be good for their immunity as well.

CONTROL OF THE THOUGHT LIFE

At 6 to 12 years of age it is time for the child to take control of their thought life. Up until age six 75%-95% of their day children live in a world of their own, they have a vivid imagination, a fantasy world.[51]

They don't think in a concrete or logical fashion. Fun games, such as "House" copying their parents, or "Doctors and Nurses", "Cops and Robbers", and "Cowboys and Indians" are very real to them.

Children at play

If you watch little children at play you will hear one say, *"Now you do this, and I will do that."* And then they go through the scenario they have set up. They continue in this vein until they tire of playing the game and move on to another.

Between ages 7 to 12 they begin to control their imagination and their ability to concentrate grows. Children with a delayed or

---

[51] Op Cit *Parenting on Purpose*

inability to concentrate can have ADD or ADHD. They may require special education to cope with learning. [52]

There is no doubt that allergies can cause misbehaviour in children and white sugar is one chemical of which to be aware. I have seen children go completely out of control when given too much sugar.

> **Life Story:** I have also been privileged to see a complete change of behaviour in a little girl who was sometimes very good and sometimes completely out of control. This reminded me of the Nursery Rhyme:
>
> *There was a little girl who had a little curl,*
>
> *Right in the middle of her forehead,*
>
> *When she was good, she was very, very good,*
>
> *And when she was bad, she was horrid.*[53]
>
> Her grandmother was led to a discovery about salicylates and the effect of these on a child's behaviour if the child was allergic to them. These salicylates are in many common foods, so grandma thought the diet was worth trying. When the girl's meals were adjusted a complete change for the better was achieved. She went from out of control to calm and obedient. It was like a miracle!

The virtue of the age 7-12 is industry. These children are learning to accomplish things, they have a deep need to please mum and dad, and this is extended to their teacher. At this age they begin to ask questions about God and the future. They begin to think in terms of life and death. They can understand the concept of heaven and the need for a Saviour.

---

[52] Attention Deficit Disorder and Attention Deficit/ Hyperactive Disorder.
[53] Henry Wadsworth Longfellow (1807-1882) American poet. This was written for his second daughter when she was a baby. Found in the *Dictionary of Quotations*, Edited by A. Norman Jeffares and Martin Grey, Pub. Harper Collins, Glasgow, 1995.

They are preparing themselves for the adult world. Purposeful parents will help them by giving them a feeling of adequacy rather than inferiority. During pre-adolescence children have a black and white mentality, they learn more compassion as they grow older.

Do not try to live through your child, rather find out their area of giftedness and personal interest and assist them in that.

By age twelve if a child has not achieved a sense of belonging through their industry, they may develop a sense of inferiority or discouragement.

If physical, mental or emotional abuse occurs at this age the child will feel intense guilt. They will feel it is their fault, they must be bad. Anxiety based disorders, fear and depression can spring from this abuse.

The virtue of pre-adolescence is personal competence. *"I can do things"*. This gives them confidence throughout their lifetime which is very important.

TEENAGERS

By the teenage years children either have learned who they are and are sure of their identity, or they will be confused if they do not feel secure in the family unit.

Education becomes more difficult, peer pressure increases, and if the emerging adult does not feel secure, they will look elsewhere to other groups for support because their need to belong is very strong. They may turn to peer groups or join gangs. Limited encouragement, a chaotic family upbringing and personal deficits will bring trouble in the teenage years.

Teenagers ask themselves these questions. *"Who am I?"* and *"Where do I belong?"*

The importance of a father

As discussed in detail in chapter four of this book the role of the father is of supreme importance.

With the younger child the father is the positive reinforcer of both the male and female identity. The absence of a father or poor fathering may produce identity confusion.

Mother love is wonderful, but a mother cannot give the same feeling of masculinity to the male child or sweet femininity to the female child that the father can give.

His authority and mystery imprints at a deep level. The virtue to be achieved at this level is fidelity, faithfulness in relationships.

If there is no father through desertion, death or divorce then it is imperative that each child has a father figure of some kind, perhaps a grandfather or an uncle who can help give the child a sense of fatherhood.

The commitment of the teenager

Parents will want their teenager to finish what they start and complete the work they commit to. If they don't then they will set themselves up for failure in life.

> *"The moving finger writes, and, having writ,*
>
> *Moves on: Nor all thy Piety nor Wit*
>
> *Shall lure it back to cancel half a Line,*
>
> *Nor all thy Tears wash out a Word of it."* [54]

---

[54] From *The Rubaiyat of Omar Khayyam*. Fitzgerald translation.

CHAPTER NINE: RELATIONSHIPS

Do not keep the alabaster boxes of your love and tenderness sealed up until your friends are dead. Fill their lives with sweetness. Speak approving, cheering words while their ears can hear them and while their hearts can be thrilled by them. (Henry Ward Beecher)[55]

MUTUALITY

To have a good relationship it is essential for a couple to blend. There should be a mutuality in all they do together. As the family grows this melding becomes more complex. The more relationships grow and develop the more need there is for give and take. Unselfishness must be the rule if families are to make beautiful music together.

In Ephesians five we see five instructions for the husband. He is -

- To love his wife sacrificially (vs. 25)
- To love her as his own body (vs. 28)
- To nourish and cherish her (vs. 33)
- He must not hate her (vs. 28-29)
- He must leave his father and mother and be united to his wife (vs.31)

Will a man die for his wife? Will he spend his life working and caring for her? During the Port Arthur massacre in Tasmania, Australia, (1996) many of the men, old and young, threw themselves over their wives to shelter them from the bullets. This

---

[55] Henry Ward Beecher (1813-1887) was an American Congregationalist clergyman, social reformer, and speaker known for his support of the abolition of slavery and his emphasis on God's love.

was seen and was noted by the authorities and newspaper reporters of the disaster.

If a man is willing to die for his wife, then she should have no trouble keeping her obligations. Paul indicates only two.

The wife's tasks

- She must be subject to her husband (vs. 22)
- She must respect her husband (vs. 33)

There is no mention in either of these lists in Ephesians of romantic love as we know it, but Paul's remarks raise the ideal of marriage to the highest level.

However, in the Old Testament we see indications of true love blossoming among Israel's young people. For example, we can read the Song of Solomon, a poem of young love and romance, the love story of Ruth and Boaz in the book of Ruth and a beautiful wedding song in Psalm 45.

From these we can see that romantic love, though not mentioned in Ephesians five, is a real and positive experience that God arranged for us to enjoy.

By contrast, in our present culture, materialism and humanism are trying to bring marriage down to the lowest level. Because of this people today give lip service to words like love, trust, and honour, but they only trust things they can see, things they can manage.

Therefore, as Christians we must sift everything we see or hear through the Word of God otherwise we will be easily influenced by the prevailing culture presented on TV, radio, newspapers, and magazines.

Ask yourself, "What does the Bible say?"

Although there are many good programmes on television, it also teaches sex outside of marriage, easy divorce, abortion, un-disciplined children, anti-heroes, and murder. It could be a force for good, a tool to build up marriages, instead it is being used to destroy morality and with it the marriage bond.

Here is the ideal attitude for a family:

> "Successful family living strikes me as being in many ways like playing in a string ensemble. Each member has his or her own skills… but the grace and strength and sweetness of the performance comes from everyone's willingness to subordinate individual skill and personal ambition to the requirement of balance and blend."[56]

The best way to live in a family is to practise unselfishness, fairness and good manners, obeying the golden rule to treat others as you would have them treat you.

COMMUNICATION IN MARRIAGE

Communication and prayer are two cornerstones of the marriage relationship so make sure you understand one another and pray together. There is a difference between the sexes in ways of communication and women especially should be aware of this. Men use report talk. *"Give me the facts, just the facts, don't waffle."* Women use rapport talk, they make friends easily and quickly become intimately acquainted with their women friends, sharing histories within hours of meeting.

In contrast men tend to go fishing together or play golf with their new acquaintances rather than share intimate details of their life. The problem is that in a marriage, women want to share their day and men just want to relax. So, the woman feels neglected because the husband doesn't want to hear about her day, and he feels disgruntled because she won't let him rest.

---

[56] https:/ampine-hearthridgereflections.com/category/annis duff.

Of course, if both are working outside the home then this scenario will be changed as both will come home tired and need to work together to prepare a meal and get the children fed and into bed.

But the truth of the matter concerning speech is if men used rapport talk (warm, fuzzy and intimate) rather than report talk (facts given in precise order) in their place of employment they would be laughed at and despised by their workmates.

MUTUAL SUBMISSION

We are told to submit to one another out of reverence for Christ. Neither should rule but together husbands and wives should work out their problems and make their decisions. There is a quality of submission the husband owes to his wife and there is a condition of submission that the wife owes to her husband. With this understood peace and love will prevail in the marriage.

This word submission is hard to understand and indeed it has been greatly distorted by some husbands who demand unquestioned submission from their wife. The truth is lack of love and mutual submission can cause God's Word to be discredited and prayers to go unanswered. Husbands should be considerate of their wife and treat her respectfully because both are equal in God's eyes.[57]

Husbands should not expect God to answer their prayers if they treat their wife as a chattel without any respect. A husband and wife together make a team. The husband who listens to his wife and respects her opinion will save himself from many a blunder, because God has given women intuition and they know instinctively who they can trust. A wife can warn her husband not to trust a certain person, perhaps saving him from a serious mistake.

---

[57] 1 Peter 3:7; Galatians 3:28

What is submission?

F.B. Meyer, a well-known theologian and author has these four things to say concerning submission which sheds some much-needed light on the subject. He maintains these four things:

> "The woman is not owned by the man nobody is owned by anybody but God.
>
> "Submission comes from the Latin "sub" (to place under). The wife belongs to her husband, and she has been placed under him for her protection. He is not to coerce her or bully her but to protect and care for her.
>
> "He is not to insist on his own way in everything but together they are to work out their problems and make decisions with God's help.
>
> "The wife should be grateful for her husband's protection, not rebellious under it."[58]

Matthew Henry, a famous Christian of the eighteenth Century, shares in his Commentary on Genesis chapter 2 these same ideas beautifully.

> "Eve was made of a rib out of the side of Adam. Not made out of his head to rule over him, nor out of his feet to be trampled on by him. But out of his side to be equal with him, under his arm to be protected, and near his heart to be beloved."[59]

Christian Maturity

Immaturity can cause much trouble in a marriage relationship. In these days of the selfish ME generation there are personality disorders which can cause havoc in family life. For instance: A passive aggressive man will constantly put off doing things he is

---

[58] Frederick Brotherton Meyer (1847-1929) Theologian and author.
[59] Matthew Henry (1662-1714) was a Non-Conformist Minister and author.

asked to do. In this way he seeks to punish his wife. He may not realise what he is doing or why, but the fact is that this behaviour can ruin his marriage. There is a more mature way to conduct your life:

> "Learning to give when we'd rather receive, forgive when we'd rather nurse a grudge and love when we'd rather be loved, moves us toward Christian maturity."[60]

This kind of unselfishness is vital for a happy marriage. It is the mature person who seeks to love and forgive when hurt by their partner.

Mature people will:

- Concentrate on learning as much as they can on having a good marriage.
- Consider their partners feelings.
- Compliment their partner.
- Communicate well with their partner.
- Keep confidentiality with their partner.

Immature people may:

- Try to control their partner.
- Try to coerce their partner.
- Be cruel to their partner.
- Selfishly constrain their partner.
- Treat their partner with contempt.

LOVE IS A VERB

Love is a doing word as well as a noun.

We should provide a climate in the home in which love, honesty and security can flourish. Love and self-control for the adults and discipline for the children should be in balance. If these are not

---

[60] Lars Grandberg, President of Northwest College Iowa.

firmly in place in a family, then material gifts will have no meaning and frustration and anger will be the result.

> "If a child is given everything he asks for, if his anxious mother always comforted him when he cried, if his minder always let him do as he wanted, then he will never be able to cope with anything unpleasant in life."[61]

Speak tactfully

People can sometimes be cruel in their speech. Both men and women can be sarcastic and brutal in their quarrels. Far better to speak good positive words that will bring blessing than cruel negative words that end in separation.

Look for one thing each day to compliment, uplift and speak well of your spouse and family members. If you follow this godly wisdom, you will go a long way to ensuring a happy healthy life for you and yours.

Making right decisions

Each day we are faced with making many decisions. Often right and wrong is very evident. Other times serious consideration and prayer is necessary to determine what is good, better, or best for our lives and the influence our decision will have upon the lives of others. Here are eleven questions, which if you answer them honestly will help you to make the right decision.

- **The personal test:** Will doing it make me a better or worse Christian?
- **The practical test**: Will doing it likely bring desirable or undesirable results?
- **The social test:** Will doing it influence others to be better or worse Christians?

---

[61] Op Cit. Seneca

- **The universal test**: Suppose everyone did it?
- **The scriptural test**: Is it expressly forbidden in the Word of God?
- **The stewardship test**: Will doing it involve a waste of God's talents invested in me?
- **The missionary test**: Will doing it help or hinder the progress of the kingdom of God on earth?
- **The character test**: Will doing it make me stronger or weaker morally?
- **The publicity test**: Would I be willing for my friends to know about it?
- **The common-sense test:** Is it good, plain, every day, ordinary common sense?
- **The family test**: Will doing it bring credit or dishonour to my family?[62]

---

[62] From the Skyline Wesleyan Church. Lemon Grove, California.

CHAPTER TEN:
THE HEALTHY FAMILY

History teaches us that there is no substitute for the family if we are to have a society that stands for human beings at their best (Ray Lyman Wilbur).[63]

THE SIGNS OF A HEALTHY FAMILY[64]

Here are the signs of a healthy family, one in which the individuals love each other, work well together, and experience the happiness this creates.

Healthy families communicate with one another and listen to one another

One of the most frequent causes of discord in a family is lack of communication. Family interaction should be open and clear. Wives complain, *"He never listens to me."* Husbands complain, *"You didn't tell me."*

As mentioned in chapter nine, men and women are different, women talk in rapport form, men in report form. In other words, men just give the facts, but the ladies give the details.

> **Life Story:** This became clear to me when, early in our married life, my husband and I took turns going to a prayer meeting each week while one of us stayed home to look after our children. When I came home, and Ken asked me how the meeting progressed he would hear a description of the whole meeting from the first chorus

---

[63] Ray Lyman Wilbur (1875 – 1949) was an American medical doctor who served as the third president of Stanford University and was the 31st United States Secretary of the Interior.

[64] Headings for this chapter were collected by Dolores Cullen from interviews with 500 counsellors on what they considered to be the signs of a happy family. The comments are my own.

to the last amen. When he went to the meeting and returned home to be asked how the meeting went his answer was invariably one word, *"Fine"*. If I wanted more I would have to dig deep and ask specific questions which he would answer patiently, but not in the detail I would have liked.

People frequently misunderstand each other because of their different life journey. Care must be taken when communicating to explain carefully what you mean and make sure the other person understands what has been said, otherwise the result of a conversation can look like this-:

What the speaker intended to say.

- What the speaker actually said.
- What the speaker thought he said.
- What the listener wanted to hear.
- What the listener actually heard.
- What the listener thought he heard.

The only way to ascertain that you have heard correctly is to repeat what you have heard back to your spouse in your own words. Then your partner can say, *"Yes, that is what I meant."* Or perhaps, *"No, that is not what I meant. I meant something quite different."* This can be explored until the satisfaction of being understood completely is obtained.

When communicating with children, parents should make sure the children understand their requests according to each child's age and understanding. Also, according to the child's temperament. Some children are less aware, more lost in their imagination than others and parents should make sure this type of child has heard their request before they lose their temper and begin shouting!

If there has been a quarrel, then reconciliation of family members should be a priority. Misunderstandings should be cleared up quickly. Resolution of conflicts for both parents and children should be worked out with wit and wisdom, not favouring one child above another.

Parents should be aware that coming home from school time is a very precious communication time. Small children who come home to a parent will be full of the day's happenings and want to share. If the parent is not there, then this precious time is lost forever. If the parent is there, then these times of communication can be prolonged through the teenage years. This will bring much joy and closeness and understanding of the child and a friendship can be developed and continued into adulthood.

Communication is not always verbal, much can be conveyed by a touch, a hug, a smile. Are you communicating well in your family? Check by asking yourself these questions.

> "Do you indulge in passive listening? That is do you ignore other members of the family when they speak.

> "Do you send double blind messages? That is do you say you love your wife but then leave her with the children all day Saturday while you play golf or tennis.

> "Do your messages have hidden, obscure or ambiguous meanings?

> "Do you use the silent treatment on a family member instead of communicating your true feelings and getting the problem out where it can be solved?

> "Do you withdraw into yourself instead of being open about your feelings?

> "Do you have unresolved anger or hostility against other members of the family?

"Do you withhold affectionate statements from other members of the family?

"Do you speak down to another member of the family?

"Do you express appreciation to other members of the family where appropriate?

"Do you use active listening when you speak to other members of the family? That is paraphrasing the other person's thoughts back to him or her.

"Do you use critical remarks? Do you use intimidating statements?"[65]

Healthy families affirm and support one another

Family members should support one another, especially in public! When a husband denigrates his wife in public, he is showing his immaturity. By downgrading her he unconsciously seeks to prove his superiority. Instead, when he insults her, he demotes himself.

The same holds true when a wife insults her husband in public, thus showing her immaturity.

If children are not encouraged but instead constantly humiliated by their parents in front of their peers, they will not forget this embarrassment. When they grow up, they will have no lasting friendship for their parents.

Husband, support your wife; wife support your husband, parents support your children, you will each reap great benefits throughout your life for this forbearance.

Healthy families teach respect for others

We must teach our children respect for authority. For if we do not then anarchy will be the eventual result for our nation. We must also

---

[65] I regret I do not remember where I obtained this list of queries.

teach them respect for those who are elderly. Other cultures have more respect for their aged family members than we do here in Australia. They do not despise the wisdom they can learn from them.

Unfortunately, the past few years have broken down much of the respect Australians had for their government members, for their police force and saddest of all for their ministers of religion. However, we must not forget that there are good men and women in all these fields. We must not be blind to the evil that exists, but as far as we are able, we should teach our children to observe and give allegiance to those who are in authority.

Healthy families learn to share

We should also teach our children respect for other people's property. This can begin when they are only small children. During those years they should have some special toys of their own that other children are not permitted to play with without their permission. Other toys can be shared. If there is more than one child in the family, then each one should have one or two special things of their own. In this way they learn to respect other children's belongings and have the joy of treasuring and taking care of things belonging exclusively to them. If their personal ownership is not respected, then they will not learn to respect the rights of others.

Healthy families develop a sense of trust

Children learn trust in the first 18 months of their life. If they do not learn it then, if instead they learn mistrust, then this can be a grave problem to them throughout their life.

How do they learn not to trust others? This happens when children are neglected or abused in some way. A sense of trust is developed by loving care of the child, by hugs and kisses, and by hearing loving voices talking to him or her.

Apart from those very important first months of a child's life trust can be built up in family life in several ways. Parents must keep their promises to their children. Don't make promises unless you are very sure you can keep them. If you make mistakes, don't be afraid to admit them.

By admitting your mistakes, you are giving the child permission to admit mistakes also. This is good for them as it helps their self-esteem to know they don't always have to be perfect.

Trust is fragile and easily lost. Teenagers should be made aware of this. If parents lose trust in their word, then it will take a long time for them to regain that trust. It is not enough for a family member to say, *"I should be forgiven,"* After all if you left someone to care for a sizeable amount of money and they spent it all on themselves you would not leave them with another large sum. They would have to prove themselves over a great while before you could trust them again.

The same holds true for husband and wife. Trust can be broken by emotional abuse, lies, adultery and constant quarrelling and these negatives are not easily repaired between couples.

Think of your marriage as a crystal vase which could be dropped and shattered and unable to be restored to its original condition. Then treat your marriage even more carefully than you would the crystal vase by showing love, kindness, honesty, faithfulness, and forbearance toward one another.

Healthy families have a sense of play and humour

Life can be sad. Our global village, through television, papers and magazines brings tales of war and misery, house invasions, stabbings, murders, and rapes. If we are not careful to protect our children from this type of news and bring instead some sense of happiness and joy into their lives, we will have depressed children and teenagers.

There are times when we must put aside the cares of this life to give our children memories of fun and laughter. Play with your children, laugh with them, take them on picnics, tell jokes and enjoy their attempts at humour, show them you love them and care about them.

Healthy families exhibit a sense of shared responsibility

Everyone in the family should share the chores as soon as they are old enough. If not, they think the chores are done by magic. One word of caution is needed here. If you ask a child to make their own bed don't come along later and remake it! This lowers a child's self-esteem. Put up with less than perfect, they will improve with age. If there are pets then they must be fed, dishes must be done, rubbish must be removed. Share the chores according to your family needs, but make sure you do not give your child a job that is beyond them, and make sure you do not load them down with too many responsibilities. Let them have some time to play, dream and just be children.

Healthy families teach a sense of right and wrong

A child who has not been brought up with a foundation of basic morality is more likely to cheat, lie and steal with no conscience sense of having done wrong because of our fallen nature without Christ.

The humanism that is being taught in our school system is reaping a whirlwind of terror and murder performed by younger and younger children. We must be consistent in the teaching of right and wrong, so our children know the difference by the time they are seven years of age.

What is the age of responsibility according to the law? Here in New South Wales a child of ten years can be put into juvenile detention, but this is under review by the government as some think this is too young.

It is interesting to look at the Jewish family for guidance here.

Jewish children have three periods of instruction. The first from their mother until they are weaned, possibly by three years of age. Then fathers take over the instruction and are responsible for the sins of their sons until they are thirteen years of age. After this year of

Bar Mitzvah, the son takes on all the responsibilities and obligations of an adult concerning the law.

For the girls their Bar Mitzvah occurs at the age of 12 years. Jewish children are taught to honour both mother and father and I am sure that mothers continue to educate their daughters and instruct them in housekeeping, cooking, sewing, and mending until they mature and decide what career or profession they wish to follow.

As mentioned before, it is a good idea to have a list of the Ten Commandments on a wall of your home so that the children can read them over and over as they grow up.

They have a strong sense of family in which rituals and traditions abound

Every family should celebrate birthdays, Christmas, and other special days that are important to them. When the children become adults and begin families of their own, they should be encouraged to begin their own times of feasting and rejoicing.

Special foods and gifts can be kept for these occasions, so they do not lose their significance. Half the fun for a child is the looking forward to special times of feasting and present giving.

Children should be given their own pocket money so they can buy or make presents for their parents and siblings. This will help them get an idea of what money is and how to manage it. If presents are bought for them to give without them having to save up first, they will grow up with a very poor idea of money management. Each family must decide for themselves how they will handle pocket money.

Healthy families have a balance of interaction among members

Children have a very strong sense of justice and fairness. They will notice if one child is preferred in the family by father or mother. This can be very hurtful to a child and he or she can become very wilful and naughty just to be noticed. To them a smack is better than no parental attention at all. The healthy family avoids favouring one child over another.

Healthy families have a shared religious core

This can add a very great strength to a family. It binds the family together. But if the children are sent to Sunday School and the parents stay at home, then the children will more than likely leave the church as soon as they are twelve years of age.

If the mother takes the children and the father stays home, then other factors come into play. The husband and father can become jealous of the church and the pastor and annoyed if the church takes too much of his wife's time, especially if she then neglects her household responsibilities.

As they grow older the children can begin to take sides and if this is so the family will have trouble. It is best to decide how you are going to deal with religious observances before marrying, if this is done the family religious life will flow more smoothly. The very best result for family happiness is for all the family members to go to church together!

Healthy families respect each other's privacy

Privacy should be respected. While the parents will expect to know all about a child in the early years this will not always continue into the teenage years. Teenagers will begin to have a life of their own and slowly grow away from their parents. They will begin to think for themselves and start making some decisions. This is a difficult time for both the teenager and the parents. A teenager can be very grown up one day and show increased maturity and the next day act in an immature manner. If parents and teenagers manage to live through this awkward time, and if a close friendship has been built up over many years, then the process will not be too painful.

Privacy is something we should all be allowed to have, but there is a balance and sometimes parents need to exercise their authority to save the teenager from danger.

Healthy families value service to others

It is a good idea to teach children to spend some time helping others. This can begin with helping the parents and then perhaps through a Community Organisation the children can participate in aiding others. Teenagers can join groups to assist the elderly and there are associations that do, "good works" in each community. Remember there is nothing like a good example. If the parents are not interested in volunteering to help in the various ways available, then it is not likely that the children will think of this kind of activity for themselves.

Healthy families foster table time and conversation

This is a dying art. Because of our busy lifestyles, and because of television, families seldom sit down to a meal together, let alone talk to one another when they do. The art of dinnertime conversation has become archaic. However, if it can be revived with some effort on the part of each member of the family, then it can have many positive results. Children can be taught many things without them being aware that they are learning.

> **Life story:** During the 2nd World War years our mother had a large map of the world on the wall of our kitchen. As the war progressed, she showed us where the fighting was going on and where our father was fighting. These family conversations conducted by our mother helped to unite our family even though one member was overseas.
>
> Dad was a Rat of Tobruk, one of the 2nd 10th Battalion, hemmed in by Rommel's forces. After the war he told us of his experiences, the food supply was so low that any soldier caught stealing food was shot immediately.

They were reduced to tinned bully beef and weevilly biscuits. They had to bang their biscuits on something to eject the weevils before they ate. My father could never again face tinned meat after he came home, 6 feet tall but a bare 7 ½ stone (105 pounds) in weight. We learned a lot about the world and the horrors of war during those dinner times, but the very worst was kept from the younger members of the family.

If the family eats together in the evenings parents can pick up on problems before they get too hard to handle. Time can be spent in communicating to one another about the day's activities and there can be shared fun and laughter. Table manners can be taught by example so that when the children are invited out for a meal, they already know the polite way to behave.

Life story. When my father came home from the war, he had a great interest in the news broadcast which came on each day at 6.00pm while we ate dinner. All five of us children had to be very quiet while he listened. I can remember him lecturing us one day, saying, "*One day there will be no countries, there will only be Companies.*" Time is slowly proving him correct as so many Companies, such as Google and Facebook now have more money than a small country.

About this time the tape recorder was invented and so my older brother decided to tape one of dad's lectures. He hid the tape recorder under the table before the evening meal and dad was the only one who did not know what was happening. Later, while we were still seated around the table and the news and dad's nightly lecture were over, Jim played back the tape. When dad heard the voice, he leaned forward and said, "Who is that?" Then he said, "He knows what he is talking about!" Then at last he realised what was happening and said, "That's me!"

He took the joke in good part, and we all had a good laugh at his expense. He continued with the nightly lectures though as he was an armchair politician, and we were his captive audience. He would have done well in parliament, but he did not have the finances or the energy to stand for a seat in government.

Healthy families share leisure time

When the children are young it is easy to spend spare time together but as they get older, around fourteen to fifteen years they begin to want to go out with their friends.

From then on it may take some ingenuity to get the family together for play times. One way this can be overcome is by making your children's friends welcome in your home as well as inviting them to go with the family on occasions.

If there has been a family tradition to spend Friday evenings together having fun as a family, then this can be continued without too much effort right through the teenage years. If this has not been a tradition, then it will be more and more difficult to spend time together as a family.

Healthy families admit to and seek help with problems

Traditionally it is the wife who is usually willing to get some help with a family problem. This is understandable because men are taught from an early age to be brave, to solve their own problems. However, in this complex world in which we live it is best to get help as soon as possible when the going gets tough. There are many good books available, and these are very helpful but there are also counsellors who are trained to assist families in trouble and to help parents to know what to do when their children are proving difficult to handle. Learn all you can and get help if needed.

THE CHRISTIAN FAMILY

The Bible does not give much instruction for the family. It doesn't need to as the instructions for the church are also applicable to the home. Each family or household is like a microcosm of the larger church, or a cell of the larger body.

Christian families love one another; forgive one another; are peaceful and thankful. They teach and admonish one another, and they do everything in the name of the Lord. **This is the ideal!**

However, it may take many years before this perfection is reached. First, the children must be raised and reach some maturity and then all members of the family must be following the Lord together for this level to be achieved. Still, it is nice to know what can be accomplished by a Christian family. Here is a scripture which gives a good description of the church and so also of the family.

> *Therefore, as God's chosen people, holy and dearly loved, clothe yourselves with compassion, kindness, humility, gentleness and patience. Bear with one another and forgive one another, if any of you has a grievance against someone. Forgive as the Lord forgave you. And over all these virtues put on love which binds them all together in perfect unity* (Colossians 3:12-14).

ADVICE FOR THE FAMILY

They strengthen, encourage and comfort one another as the Holy Spirit strengthens and encourages and comforts the church. (1 Corinthians 14:2)

They bear one another's burdens (Galatians 6:2)

They know and recognise the wisdom that comes from God (James 3:17).

They don't let the sun go down while they are still angry, they make sure to reconcile with one another quickly (Ephesians 4:26).

Mothers and fathers submit to one another because they love God and revere their Saviour and children obey and honour their parents (Ephesians 5:21 & 6:1-3).

Christian fathers don't sow bitterness and anger into their children, but instead they strengthen, encourage and comfort them (Ephesians 6:4).

What a perfect family this would be if all these words of wisdom were followed diligently. These families would be able to withstand any attack from our modern culture or from enemies of the Christian way of living.

CHAPTER ELEVEN: THE DYSFUNCTIONAL FAMILY

For those who will fight bravely and not yield, there is triumphant victory over all the dark things of life (James Allen).[66]

WITHOUT NATURAL AFFECTION

But mark this: There will be terrible times in the last days. People will be lovers of themselves, lovers of money, boastful, proud, abusive, disobedient to their parents, ungrateful, unholy, without love, unforgiving, slanderous, without self-control, brutal, not lovers of the good, treacherous, rash, conceited, lovers of pleasure rather than lovers of God - having a form of godliness but denying its power (Timothy 3:1-5)

There are so many troubled families today and this has been true for many years. There are numerous instances of a father killing his wife and children or of a father killing himself and his children and leaving his former wife to grieve. Here is a quote from a book printed in 2002 which shows even then a callous attitude and a lack of natural affection from a young man who should have been a protector and provider for his wife and coming baby.

> The husband, a chronic womanizer, shot and killed his seven-month pregnant wife because she was going to leave him after giving him an ultimatum about his latest extra marital affair. The reason? He did not want to pay maintenance.[67]

---

[66] James Allen was a British philosophical writer known for his inspirational books and poetry and as a pioneer of the self-help movement. He was the author of the book, *As a Man Thinketh*.
[67] *It's called Survival*, by Barbara Adams, Hyde Park Press; Richmond, S.A. 2002

There are many troubled families these days for various reasons. Selfish, unforgiving, lacking self-control, seemingly without natural love for their spouse or children. A person without any fear of God cares only about themselves and what they want.

Not having any firm basis for living, such as the Judeo/Christian foundation they do whatever seems right in their own eyes. In doing so they can reap a whirlwind of unhappiness and the despair of broken relationships.

Much of the evil in our culture today stems from the fact that people in general have no belief in or fear or reverence for the God of the Bible. They do not believe he is a holy God, the final judge of what we do in this life. Without this restraint there has been a gradual descent into more and more sexual perversion. God has warned in the Bible of the results of multiple sexual encounters which can result in disease and eventual death.

TYPES OF THE TROUBLED FAMILY [68]

Verbal emotional abuse

Ignoring a child by not listening, or not responding. Giving a child two choices which are both negative, or constantly projecting blame onto a child, continually growling, never praising.

Distorting a child's sense of reality by saying untruthful things. Such as, *"Your brother isn't on drugs. He's just having a hard time; you are imagining things."*

Blaming others for a child's problems – never teaching the child to take responsibility for their own actions or mistakes.

Communicating confused double messages to a child, *"Yes, I love you, now don't bother me, can't you see I'm busy!"*

---

[68] I thank Dr. DeKoven for permission to use his notes on the Dysfunctional Family and Co-Dependency. The life stories added are my own.

Overprotecting a child. Hovering over them, never letting them play rough. Every child needs some dirt!

> **Life story:** Overprotection was displayed by Margaret, a mother who had only one child and despaired of being able to have any other children. She hovered over her child like a mother hen with one little chicken, not allowing him to play any rough games or climb trees with other boys. This attitude could be mistaken for loving care on her part, but it became emotional abuse when the child became increasingly nervous and anxious. He began to think the world a dangerous place and that he could not take care of himself. It took away his courage to try new things and grow and mature properly.

Perfectionism

A perfectionist is often angry because they can't live up to their own inadequacies. They continually procrastinate because they don't want to finish something which may not then be perfect. They are angry at their own children for the same reason. They remind them of their own inadequacies.

Verbal rebukes, correction, disapproving scowls, and critical harping are some of the ways perfectionists will speak to their children. Their conversation is sprinkled with 'should' and 'ought'.

This is verbal torture and the child thinks, *"Why try, I'll never be good enough!"*

A child brought up under this regime will eventually rebel. Balance is the key that produces healthy children who can make healthy choices.

> **Life story:** Robert and Meg were average parents who tried to strike a balance between positive and negative ways of dealing with their children. Through the help of

a counsellor and trial and error they found it was better to reward good behaviour and ignore bad conduct. Especially when their children misbehaved because they were overtired or hungry. They developed a family word "hangry" which meant "angry because hungry".

They learned children don't always understand why they are irritable and naughty but that they, as parents, could work out the reasons and sometimes make allowances. That positive reinforcement, rewarding good behaviour, was the way to go as punishment for bad behaviour only emphasized what had been done and guaranteed it would be done again if the naughty child was hungry, tired or just yearning for attention.

They learned one last important lesson from the counsellor. If the parent is always growling when things go wrong and offers no praise when things go right, then the child will give up trying to please their parent. Balance between the positive and the negative is the way to go. These lessons were a great help to Robert and Meg and guaranteed a much happier family life for them and their children.

Rigidity

Some families follow unbending rules, they have a super strict family lifestyle and a legalistic belief system. They never give in or change their mind on anything.

In all they have an over rigid, negative family experience. Relationships and events are strictly controlled.

Joy and spontaneity are smothered by responsibility and duty. – *"We don't ever do that" "Don't ever do anything to embarrass our family." "No, we can't change our schedule."*

> **Life story:** Harry and Pat would stop their car on the way to an invite to dinner and lecture their children on

behaving just so while they were visiting. They did not want their children to put a foot wrong. Woe to them if they misbehaved! Punishment would be forthcoming on arriving home at the slightest misdoing causing embarrassment to their parents.

This kind of control leaves negative memories for children of strict parents.

Silence

"We don't share family secrets. We don't ask for help if we have a problem."

Children are sworn to forced silence they grow up believing they must handle the burdens of life by themselves – they can never ask for counsel.

Repression

Identifying and expressing emotions in a positive way is healthy. Over controlling and repressing them is asking for future difficulty. - *"Don't cry" "Be brave." "Stop that."*

Repression becomes a death sentence for any future relationships, such as marriage. So, currently men are trying to get back in touch with their feelings which were stifled in childhood.

When we repress emotions, we are denying reality, this leads to physical problems such as compulsive behaviours and eating disorders.

Feelings don't go away if we repress them, they just dam up. Eventually the dam will crack and burst, and the emotions will explode unchecked, usually in a harmful way. Therefore, most quarrels are over little things, seemingly ridiculous!

> **Life story:** In Tanya's dysfunctional family her father never allowed tears because, to him, tears were a sign of weakness. So, her normal feelings became distorted into

rage, an emotion her father approved because it reflects strength. Now whenever Tanya is sad, disappointed, discouraged, or hurt, instead of having a good healthy cry, she throws an angry fit. Her true feelings have been twisted. Her compulsive anger is merely a symptom of an unmet need. She doesn't really feel her fear. She doesn't really feel her loneliness. She doesn't really feel her sadness or rejection. They are all funnelled into anger, which manifests itself as bitterness, criticism, dissatisfaction, and abuse toward herself and everyone else. She will make her family's life a misery unless she can get help from a psychiatrist.

Triangulation

In triangulation the parents use the child as a go-between. The child is caught in the middle and is being used in an unhealthy way. Children used like this think it is normal until they see another family talking and showing affection toward one another. If this becomes a regular pattern, the child may become a guilt collector, feeling responsible for everything that goes wrong in the family.

> **Life story:** Joan spent years being a go between for her parents who refused to talk to each other and lived in total silence due to unresolved problems. She cheerfully took the words spoken by her mother to her father and then took the answer from her father back to her mother and so on. As she grew into her teenage years, she discovered to her astonishment that in other families the father and mother spoke directly to one another and showed affection toward each other.

Lack of fun

Some families are too serious, and place too many burdens on their children. In this family there are no games, no jokes, or fun times to look back on in future years.

When these children become teenagers, they may be slow to mature because they need to live through those missed years and catch up on the fun of which they were robbed.

> **Life story**: A doer is a very busy individual who provides most of the maintenance functions of the family. Often doers feel tired, isolated, ignored, and used. Elaine told me she felt like she had been a parent most of her life. Being the eldest of seven children she was given adult responsibilities at an early age. Now that she is married her husband complains that she is too serious and isn't any fun to be around. Heroes like Elaine eventually burn out.

> "Remember that caregivers who do not take care of themselves eventually burn out…but putting the self-care into practice can be very difficult unless some outside person helps the family monitor what they are feeling and how they are coping."[69]

Martyrdom

Martyrdom is produced by a distorted sense of self-denial. These people have a higher tolerance for personal abuse and pain.

The parents tell their children, *"Others must always come first, no matter what the cost."*

> **Life story:** In the early days of our ministry the phone often rang during our evening meal. Because of our dedication to ministry my husband would leave his meal and rush off to help the caller. We learned in time that

---

[69] *Christian Counseling Third Edition* by Gary R. Collins, PhD; Published by Thomas Nelson. 2007. Pp.647

problems do not always come suddenly and that solutions can wait to a more appropriate time. [70]

The children often grow up seeing their parents punish themselves through overwork, eating disorders, and substance abuse. They see themselves as victims.

Entanglement

Families that have a too close emotional entanglement are dysfunctional.

Individual identities become blurred and diminished. If one member is depressed, then all are depressed and so on.

BEWARE OF CO-DEPENDENCY

This is an irrational involvement with another party where denial, imbalance, disruptive behaviours, and low self-esteem shape the relationship.

The co-dependent person is usually driven by an intense need to connect with and a deep desire to belong to a significant other (person, object, system, or entity), yet at the same time is compelled by an unconscious motive to control the outcomes of that relationship. The person usually has a great need to smooth conflicts and tensions.

- To rescue those in trouble.
- To avoid embarrassment and shame.
- To readily fix problematic situations.
- To control outside events.
- To take full responsibility for people's actions and behaviours.
- To constantly try to keep the peace or harmony at any price.

---

[70] For more on this subject see, *Unsung Heroines* 3rd Edition (2019) Pp. 19 under the heading, *Intrusion*.

CHAPTER TWELVE: BUILDING A SUCCESSFUL FAMILY.

Life can only be understood backwards, but it must be lived forwards. (Soren Kierkegaard)[71]

PROBLEMS AND SOLUTIONS

The problem we are facing today, with the divorce rate rising to an all-time high, is caused by lack of knowledge of the real love needed when two people begin their married life together.

Even Christian people are floundering because of the lack of good role models in their lives. Many husbands do not understand how to be a good husband. The wife doesn't realise how to be a good wife. Neither one knows how to be a good parent. Confused and bewildered they are searching for answers.

There is a vital need for a good foundation for a happy married life, for learning how to relate together and, with God's help, for bringing up children successfully.

Common-sense

Common sense would indicate that romantic love is not a good foundation for marriage. A couple should rely, not on an emotional experience, but on the realistic need to choose a partner that fits into one's own social level, personal expectations, and mutual goals. Having worked out these important points together a couple can then proceed to allow each other to "fall in love".

Before a young man or woman follow their hormones, they should think carefully. The young man should ask, "Does this young lady come from a similar background to myself? Is she as well educated, does she have similar likes and dislikes? What religion, if any, does

---

[71] Soren Kierkegaard (1813-1855) Danish philosopher and theologian; founder of existentialism.

she follow? What are her hobbies? Is she industrious or lazy? What are her parents like? How does she speak to her parents? Is she well-mannered and kind?"

And the young woman should ask herself the same questions about her young man.

If you are willing to settle for less than this, then you have a problem with your own self- image! If you are to learn to love your spouse with a free and happy love, then you must learn to love yourself first.

Loving yourself you will take care of yourself, work to feed and clothe yourself and keep yourself mentally and spiritually healthy. If you do these things, then you will be able to find ways to love and care for your spouse.

Indeed, to have a truly tranquil life, and a happy marriage without strife it is best to pray earnestly together and then follow God's guidance. For instance, if you always endeavour to bring happiness to your spouse, you should receive happiness in return. If you trust God to help you to understand and appreciate your spouse then he will, because God cares for you both and wants your marriage to be successful.

> *Trust in the Lord with all your heart and lean not on your own understanding: in all your ways submit to him, and he will make your paths straight* (Proverbs 3:5-6).

Who should command?

> **Life Story.** In the 50's family shows on television showed happy families with strong fathers and happy wives and mothers. How this has changed! Slowly but surely many of the family shows have degenerated until the fathers are portrayed as weak bumbling fools and the mother as the strong common-sense bulwark of the family. The very clever Elon Musk will not allow his children to watch *The Simpsons* as this programme illustrates the modern trend of a bumbling fool of a

husband and father controlled by his wife. This and many other similar scenarios have caused much harm to families in these days of the 21st century. Many men are angry and have learned to despise women who look down on them and laugh at them. This is not God's intention for the family, far from it.

Now many find it difficult to understand who should be in command in a marriage. The truth is neither should be in command! In God's word we read that he made Eve to be a helpmeet for Adam because together, a man and a woman can express all the qualities of God.

God created man in his own image, in the image of God he created them; male and female he created them (Genesis 1:27).

The Lord God said, "It is not good for the man to be alone. I will make a helper suitable for him" (Genesis 2:18).

Man and woman together in a marriage contract complete God's creation. God gave us families for strength and support. Usually, a woman has intuition and perception, and a man has a logical, rational way of thinking, Together, as a team, they can work out their problems and make good decisions. Wise persons will listen to their marriage partner. A man and a woman should complete each other not compete against one another.

If you are a Christian husband, then your wife is a gift from the Lord. If you are a Christian wife, then your husband is a gift from God. Complement one another. There should be no competition, together you are a whole unit.

SACRIFICE

Submission is not something taken by the husband, but something given to him by his wife. Why? Because he loves her enough to die for her! As I mentioned earlier in this book, in a massacre in Tasmania when a gunman killed thirty-five people and wounded many more, it was very moving to read how many of the men, no matter what their age, young or old, tried to protect his wife from the gunman. Some succeeded, some did not, but they tried, and in trying they were fulfilling scripture, even though they may not have realised it.

> *Husbands, love your wives, just as Christ loved the church and gave himself up for her* (Ephesians 5:25a).

Nevertheless, someone must make the final decisions for a family, and this should be the husband, as it is his responsibility under God. However, if he is wise, he will not make any major decision without first listening to what his wife has to say about the matter. It is true that men excel in logic, but women are intuitive and sometimes they sense something is not right, or someone is not to be trusted. A sensible man will listen to his wife if she is uneasy about a decision.

Of course, there are many choices to be made each day and it would not be practical for the husband to decide every little ruling. However, those choices that affect the whole family in a radical way should be his. As pointed out in *Baker's Dictionary of Practical Theology* there should be a balance in the decision making within the family, depending on the circumstances at the time.

> "There is the question of leadership. Over concern with the idea of equality may lead to a marital stalemate when leadership is confused with superiority or dominance. There is a natural balance between partners, and the dominant one, whether man or woman, may or may not be the defined leader of the home. It makes little difference so long as both partners can agree and collaborate in leadership

responsibilities. Otherwise, there is either a covert and overt competition, or mutual deference with the frustrating failure of either one to make even everyday decisions".[72]

One of the most important aspects of marriage is good old fashioned courtesy. It is a good idea, as far as manners are concerned, to treat your spouse as you would treat a friend. For instance, you would be careful of the way you spoke to your friends, and you would be careful not to hurt their feelings because you want to keep their friendship.

Having said all these things, it is well to remember also that the marriage relationship is only for this life. Eventually, as Christians we must all stand by ourselves before the Bema, the judgment seat of Christ. Because of this your marriage relationship should not come before your relationship to God. A husband cannot demand that his wife do something that is contrary to Scripture or something that is against her conscience, and vice versa.

In all things let unselfishness be your rule. In many ways a family is a picture of the church and of Jesus' relationship to the church. Let him be your example! Jesus said,

> *My command is this: Love each other as I have loved you. Greater love has no one than this: to lay down one's life for one's friends* "(John 15:12-13).

In the past, a man did lay down his life for his wife and family over many years by working hard each day. Especially in those manual jobs which took a toll on his bodily strength. However, these days if the wife is also working outside the home this idea is blurred and no longer seen clearly because the wife also works hard, perhaps harder than her husband as she still has her home to take care of. Especially

---

[72] Turnbull, Ralph G. (Editor) *Baker's Dictionary of Practical Psychology;* Baker Book House; Grand Rapids; MI. pg. 220.

if she receives little or no help from her husband.

Remember, Love is a verb

Provide a climate in the home in which love, trust, honesty, and security can flourish. If you don't have this, then all the material things you provide will have little meaning. Instead, they will bring frustration and anger. Trust and tenderness are fragile, they cannot survive battering and bruising. People will withdraw if they are hurt. Home must be a place where family members can give unconditional love without being hurt or taken advantage of. Remember love is a verb. You can't say you love someone and then act as if you do not!

One of history's most famous families was that of Samuel and Susannah Wesley. They were parents of nineteen children, among them were John and Charles Wesley. Susannah has often been held up as an example of Christian motherhood.

Of course, we must remember that in her position as the wife of a Church of England clergyman Susannah would have had at least a cook and a maid as well as a handyman for the garden. We must not suppose that a modern wife without these helps could manage as well as Susannah was able.

> "A woman of fine intellect and good education; ruled her house with singular diligence, system and piety. The children who survived infancy were taught individually and punctiliously in the home, Mrs Wesley doing most of the teaching. A woman of methodical and systematic habits, of loving Christian character. A tender mother and a good pastor's wife. Her piety and devotion and Christian character were implanted in the lives of her children."[73]

---

[73] Moyer, Elgin S. *Wycliffe Biographical Dictionary of the Church*. Note: Wesley Susannah (1669-1742); Moody Press; Chicago.

It is interesting to note that many mothers, in view of the increasing secularisation of Government Schools, have returned to the concept of teaching their children in the home, and with a marked degree of success. I have observed a special double bond between such mothers and their children as the child looks to the mother not only for love and nurture but also for instruction and knowledge.

NON-CHRISTIAN PARTNERS

If you are married to a non-Christian, then you must accept them as they are. Pray for him. Pray for her. If Jesus can change you then he can change your spouse; but remember, to do this he first may have to change you in some way.

Be aware of and deal quickly with hurts, bitterness, criticism, and jealousy. If these are left to fester, then they may grow into insurmountable obstacles to a couple's happiness as we are advised in the book of Hebrews.

> *See to it that no one falls short of the grace of God and that no bitter root grows up to cause trouble and to defile many* (Hebrews 12:15).

A Christian wife of an unbelieving husband must try harder to be a better wife, a better housewife, and a better lover, because some unbelieving husbands are jealous of God and the church. They feel they are taking too much of their wife's time and attention. The Christian wife must be careful to keep a balance between home and church.

A Christian husband of an unbelieving wife must try harder also to take care of his wife and not to neglect her for endless meetings. He must also keep a balance.

> *Who is wise and understanding among you? Let them show it by their good life, by deeds done in the humility that comes from wisdom* (James 3:13).

How can you love in a situation such as this? You can do it by looking to the source of love. God himself will teach you. If indeed your love for your spouse has grown cold then begin to act as though you love, ask God to guide you and you will begin to see him work. What begins as an act of love can grow into a genuine resurgence of love for your spouse, partly because you have begun to reflect the love of Jesus.

> *And we all, who with unveiled faces contemplate the Lord's glory are being transformed into his image with ever increasing glory, which comes from the Lord, who is the Spirit* (2Corinthians 3:18).

In other words, the Lord of glory can change us slowly but surely into the image of Christ who died for us that we might live in eternity with him. As he does this, we can reflect his love, his gentleness, his caring, his honesty, his integrity until we grow up into the fullness of what he has begun in us.

Take this advice from a successful wife whose husband has achieved great things for God's kingdom.

> "A wife's job is not to convert her husband but to love him. God does the converting"[74].

And of course, the reverse holds true for the husband!

---

[74] A quote from Ruth Graham the wife of Evangelist Billy Graham.

CHAPTER THIRTEEN: CONCLUSIONS

The highest happiness on earth is in marriage. Every man who is happily married is a successful man even if he has failed in everything else (William Lyon Phelps)[75]

THE WORKING WIFE

The ideal way of life, at least while the children are small is for the mother to be at home to bond with them, but if this is impossible and she must work then some careful decisions will have to be made.

A decision as to who budgets the money earned and pays the bills should be worked out. This can be either husband or wife, whoever has the time and is most gifted in money matters seems to be the sensible solution to this problem.

If the wife does all the domestic tasks as well as going out to work, then she will feel resentful and grow tired and distressed. If a sensible husband assists his wife, she will have more energy to attend to his needs and he will feel more loved. The sensible decision is for a couple to work out a fair division of domestic tasks or else budget for some help in the home, even if only for a few hours per week.

If both are working, thought should also be given to spending quality time alone together on a regular basis. This is very important, especially as children are born into the family and life grows ever more hectic.

As the children grow older, they can contribute by doing their chores. If they are not required to do anything toward the smooth running of the household, then they will grow up thinking all the work is done by invisible means.

---

[75] William Lyon Phelps (1865–1943) was an American author, critic and scholar.

Train your children

> The family is an instrument in God's hands for the training of children in his ways. To accept this is to bring up your children as children of God.
>
> "It is the family spirit, the domestic godliness which forms the children to God. If this is wanting, then all that you may do beside will be as likely to annoy as to bless."[76]

One of the first things parents discover in their children is original sin! Babies begin as such sweet, adorable bundles but by the second year they are becoming disobedient and fractious. Selfishness and wilful rebellion are all too apparent. Sometimes parents do confuse tiredness with temper, and it is a good thing to watch your child carefully, to look ahead and to avoid confrontations, such as when the child is weary and ready for a nap.

Most children show mixed behaviour, sometimes they are loving and kind, sometimes greedy or disobedient. They need to grow and mature in the same way their parents did. Growing in grace is a life-time exercise.

Christian parents should begin to pray for their children even before conception. They enter by faith into a covenant relationship with God in establishing a home and family. They should entrust their children to God before birth, then from the moment of birth the children are regarded as belonging to him. By godly example and teaching, Christians should accept the responsibility of bringing up their children in the nurture, discipline, and instruction of the Lord.

Those who adopt can also believe God for their children.

Children of Christian parents can be converted at an early age and then have several re-dedications as they grow older. Some may not

---

[76] Bushnell Horace (1802-1876) *Christian Nurture*

be able to remember the exact moment of conversion, they just know they belong to God. Children cannot be expected to have the same consciousness of sin as an adult would have. If your child does accept Christ as Saviour then care must be taken not to boast of this, it is a private matter and should not be talked about to everyone, or at least not until the child is ready.

In daily conversation with your children, you should endeavour not to provoke them to anger.

> *Fathers do not exasperate your children; instead bring them up in the training and instruction of the Lord* (Ephesians 6:4).

You should not continuously nag and scold your children thus making them angry and resentful. Loving discipline, suggestions, and godly advice are the weapons for training your children in the ways of God. You will find rewards go a long way in training a young child. Incentives make obedience a pleasure whereas constant scolding makes life miserable.

> "Children must learn obedience, a lifelong socialisation process. The family is the source of learning about the necessity for negotiation and compromise between the needs and desires of the individual and the needs and desires of those around him. The parental sub-system has the task of providing a sense of belonging and personal value and setting necessary limits in such a way that children do not become overly frustrated or resentful and alienated from the family."[77]

Parents should always trust their children, at least until reason is given to do otherwise, then of course it is up to the child to regain its parent's trust. If children sense they are not trusted, then feelings of resistance and eventual rebellion will surface.

---

[77] Benner, David G. & Hill, Peter C., Editors. *Baker Encyclopedia of Psychology;* Baker Books; Grand Rapids MI.

One of the worst things parents can do is to be continually rude to their children.

> "(Sometimes) mothers and fathers treat their grown-up children with an incivility, which, offered to any other young people, would simply have terminated the acquaintance."[78]

Children learn their manners from their parents. If the parents are unfailingly courteous to each other and to their children, then the children will learn constant courtesy also and this will continue into maturity.

DISCIPLINE AND AUTHORITY

Parents need the wisdom of Solomon! They must seek to be firm and kind and at the same time fair in dealing with their children, while considering the well-being of others in the family. There must be a balance between discipline and exasperating your children.

When correcting a child, parents must take care that they are not basing their correction on what other people think or say rather than what God has said. It is fatal for the child to get the impression that it is not love motivating the discipline measured out, but what other people will think of the family if they get into trouble. If this is the case the child will feel unloved and rebellious and is more likely to offend.

> "They should be careful also to present Christianity as a faith that is exciting, robust, and intelligent. Not just a constant, unending programme of religious meetings and hymn singing. They should rather share with their children the wonders and the beauties of the creation God has made for them and the love and care of his Father heart. Children will always view God through the character of their earthly father. If he has been loving, kind and scrupulously fair, even though occasionally he

---

[78] Lewis, C. S. *The Four Loves* Fontana Books, Collins, Great Britain.

may make a mistake in his dealings with them, then they will be able to view God as being loving and kind and fair also."[79]

Parents should make time for their children and show an interest in their daily pursuits. If they do so from infancy onwards then a good relationship will be established for the years when peer pressure begins to take its toll. It is good for children to feel that their parents are also their friends.

WHAT ABOUT DIVORCE?

Though divorce is a terrible thing sometimes there is no other way to protect the wife and children from violence. Each case should be decided individually and then only after marriage counselling has been sincerely tried by both husband and wife.

Years ago, the Quebec assembly of Catholic Bishops issued a remarkable sixty-page document titled *"Heritage of Violence"*. The bishops admitted, *"There are cases where the marriage bond no longer makes any sense"*. The document is being sent to all priests and general church staff in Quebec as a guide on how to deal with victims of family violence.

> One Catholic sociologist, who asked that his name not be used said, *"I've been told that some priests would warn battered wives threatening to leave their husband that they would go to hell if they broke their marriage vows and ended the marriage."*[80]

The Christian view must be a humane one. No wife or little child should be subjected to constant violence and abuse. God has shown the way to a cheerful marriage where children can be brought up in an atmosphere of peace and happiness. It is up to each family to walk in the ways of God and not in the ways of this world.

---

[79] Inchley, John; *All About Children*.
[80] Article in *The Christian Century*; Jan.31st 1990.

But it is true that children whose parents are divorced suffer from a lack of security. Even children of loving, happy parents have friends whose parents are divorced, and they can be secretly worried that perhaps this may happen to their own parents.

> "Divorce is not an experience from which a sensitive person easily recovers. Residual emotional scars may be lifelong and contribute to emotional warping in the next generation."[81]

Sometimes parents stay together for appearances even though they want a divorce. This is very distressing and upsetting for a child. The constant quarrelling leaves emotional scars which can never be erased completely from the memory. The Samaritans, a phone service for people needing help, have had calls from children as young as eight years, but even a young baby of six-nine months knows when its parents are fighting and unhappy.

Conclusion.

The safest and best basis for a happy family life is a Christian one. Remember, always, true practical love, courtesy, common sense, trust, fairness, honesty, and security are the ideal. If these virtues are in abundant supply in family life, then happiness will abound. Husband, wife, and children will all be content.

---

[81] Ibid

CHAPTER FOURTEEN: WISDOM FROM HISTORY

Life travels upward in spirals. He who takes pains to search the shadows of the past below us, then, can better judge the tiny arc up which he climbs, more surely guess the dim curves of the future above him (Andre Gide).[82]

LEARN FROM THE PAST

We can learn much wisdom from the histories of famous people. The growth of their character, the problems they faced, and their accomplishments all furnish us with knowledge and understanding if we search for it diligently.

It does us good to read of these great men and women of history and see the mistakes they made and the triumphs they enjoyed. The truths we learn from them can improve our own understanding of what builds a good character.

I have recently been reading the biographies of Benjamin Franklin and Abraham Lincoln. They were both good men who wanted to live righteously, and both had their own system of getting rid of sin and acquiring righteousness. But we cannot change ourselves. Instead, when we believe in him God gives us his righteousness.

BENJAMIN FRANKLIN (1706-1790).

Benjamin Franklin was an American printer and publisher, author, inventor, scientist and diplomat. Here is a quote from this great man, revealing his ideas of improving and reforming himself.

> "It was about this time I conceived the bold and arduous project of arriving at moral perfection. I wished to live without committing any fault at any

---

[82] André Paul Guillaume Gide was a French author and winner of the Nobel Prize in Literature (in 1947).

time; I would conquer all that either natural inclination, custom or company might lead me into. As I knew, or thought I knew, what was right and wrong, I did not see why I might not always do the one and avoid the other. But I soon found I had undertaken a task of more difficulty than I had imagined. While my care was employed in guarding against one fault, I was often surprised by another; habit took the advantage of inattention; inclination was sometimes too strong for reason. I concluded at length, that the mere speculative conviction that it was in our interest to be completely virtuous, was not sufficient to prevent our slipping; and that the contrary habits must be broken, and good ones acquired and established, before we can have any dependence on a steady, uniform rectitude of conduct. For this purpose, I therefore contrived the following method."[83]

His list of virtues:

- Temperance – eat not to dullness, drink not to elevation.
- Silence – Speak not but what may benefit others or yourself; avoid trifling conversation.
- Order – Let all things have their places; Let each part of your business have it's time.
- Resolution – Resolve to perform what you ought; perform without fail what you resolve.
- Frugality – Make no expense but to do good to others or yourself; that is waste nothing.
- Industry – Lose no time, be always employed in something useful; cut off all unnecessary actions.

---

[83] Benjamin Franklin FRS FRSA FRSE [1706–1790] was an American polymath who was active as a writer, scientist, inventor, statesman, diplomat, printer, publisher and political philosopher.

- Sincerity – Use no hurtful deceit; think innocently and justly, and if you speak, speak accordingly.
- Justice – Wrong none by doing injuries or omitting the benefits that are your duty.
- Moderation – Avoid extremes; forbear resenting injuries so much as you think they deserve.
- Cleanliness – Tolerate no uncleanliness, in body, clothes, or habitation.
- Tranquillity – Be not disturbed at trifles, or at accidents common or unavoidable.
- Chastity – Rarely use venery (sexual relations) but for health or offspring, never to dullness, weakness, or the injury or another's peace or reputation.
- Humility – Imitate Jesus or Socrates.

"My intention being to acquire the habitude of all these virtues, I judged it would be well not to distract my attention by attempting the whole at once, but to fix on one of them at a time; and, when I should be master of that then to proceed to another, and so on, until I should have gone through the thirteen…I made a little book, in which I allotted a page for each of the virtues. I ruled each page with red ink, so as to have seven columns, one for each day of the week, marking each column with a letter for the day…I might mark, by a little black spot, every fault I found upon examination to have been committed respecting the virtue upon that day.

"I entered upon the execution of this plan for self-examination and continued it with occasional intermissions for some time. I was surprised to find myself so much more full of faults than I had imagined; but I had the satisfaction of seeing them diminish. To avoid the trouble of renewing now and then my little book, which, by scraping out the marks on the paper of old faults to make room for new ones in a new course, became full of holes, I transferred my tables and precepts to the ivory leaves of a memorandum book, on which the lines were drawn with red ink, that made a durable stain, and on those lines I marked my faults with a black led pencil, which marks I could easily wipe out with a wet sponge…

"My scheme of order gave me the most trouble… this article cost me so much painful attention, and my faults in it vexed me so much, and I made so little progress in amendment, and had such frequent relapses, that I was almost ready to give up the attempt, and content myself with a faulty character in that respect."[84]

This illustration reminded me straight away of Paul's despairing cry in Romans.

> *"So, I find this law at work. Although I want to do good, evil is right there with me. For in my inner being I delight in God's law; but I see another law at work in me, waging war against the law of my mind and making me a prisoner of the law of sin at work within me. What a wretched man I am! Who will rescue me from this body that is subject to death? Thanks be to God, who delivers me through Jesus Christ our Lord!"* (Romans 7: 21-25).

Benjamin Franklin should have realised that we cannot accomplish our own righteousness but must come to God and throw ourselves on his mercy. His grace is sufficient for us, we do not have to strive to be good but rely on the Lord to do the work.

Paul's victorious shout in Romans 8:1 says it all.

---

[84] ibid

> *"Therefore, there is now no condemnation for those who are in Christ Jesus, because through Christ Jesus the law of the Spirit of life set me free from the law of sin and death."*

Notice the past tense. This verse does not say, *"will set me free"* but, *"set me free"*.

The work is done! From now on the word is not "do" (keeping the law) but "done" (Jesus has done it for us).

What have I learned from the life of Benjamin Franklin:-

I have learned from the mistakes made by Benjamin Franklin. He tried to overcome his faults in his own strength. But the truth is that when we believe in the work Jesus did for us on the cross then sin has no more power over us, and we can begin to do good things in life without any struggle. First, we believe God has given us his righteousness by faith and then we are set free to live a life of freedom to accomplish great things for him.

DOCTOR PAUL TOURNIER (1898-1986)

Dr. Paul Tournier was a Swiss physician and author who worked with the Red Cross in the First World War. In 1932 he encountered the Oxford Group. This organisation was a Christian one founded by Frank Buchman, an American Lutheran minister. Buchman believed that all problems were the personal problems of fear and selfishness. The commitment of the members to Jesus Christ and to each other brought Dr. Paul Tournier to a new experience of living faith. He developed the idea of the '*medicine of the person*' and wrote several books on holistic medicine; that is on the relationship between the body and the spirit, in his practice. His books sold millions of copies in sixteen languages. His best books were *Guilt and Grace*, *The Meaning of Persons*, *The Person Reborn* and *To Understand Each Other*.

Studying the life of Dr Tournier and reading his books will give you an interesting insight into his thinking. He is very balanced and wise in his understanding of what God wants from us. Some Christians want an easy path to heaven with no trials, but Dr. Tournier cuts through this attitude and lets us know that we need to take up our cross daily and be led by God, trusting in his direction for our life. However, it is only in looking back over the years that we can clearly see God's guiding hand. The most important lesson of our Christian life is to put our full trust in the Lord and not lean on our own strength. No matter what trials overtake us we can trust him fully to bring our life through to a victorious conclusion when it is our time to go to be with him.

> *Trust in the Lord with all your heart and lean not on your own understanding; in all your ways submit to him and he will make your paths straight* (Pr 3:5-6).

Here are some of his quotes:-

1. We are nearly always longing for an easy religion, easy to understand and easy to follow; a religion with no mystery, no insoluble problems, no snags; a religion that would allow us to escape from our miserable human condition; a religion in which contact with God spares us all strife, all uncertainty, all suffering and all doubt; in short, a religion without a cross.

2. God leads us step by step, from event to event. Only afterward, as we look back over the way we have come and reconsider certain important moments in our lives in the light of all that has followed them, or when we survey the whole progress of our lives, do we experience the feeling of having been led without knowing it, the feeling that God has mysteriously guided us.

3. Christian faith does not involve repressing one's anxiety in order to appear strong. On the contrary, it means recognizing one's weakness, accepting the inward truth

about oneself, confessing one's anxiety, and still to believe, that is to say that the Christian puts his trust not in his own strength, but in the grace of God.

4. For the fulfilment of his purpose God needs more than priests, bishops, pastors, and missionaries. He needs mechanics and chemists, gardeners and street sweepers, dressmakers and cooks, tradesmen, physicians, philosophers, judges, and shorthand typists ... I do not serve God only in the brief moments during which I am taking part in a religious service, or reading the Bible, or saying my prayers, or talking about him in some book I am writing or discussing the meaning of life with a patient or a friend. I serve him quite as much when I am giving a patient an injection, or lancing an abscess, or writing a prescription, or giving a piece of good advice. Or again I serve him quite as much when I am reading the newspaper, travelling, laughing at a joke, or soldering a joint in an electric wire. I serve him by taking an interest in everything, because he is interested in everything, because he has created everything and has put me in his creation so that I might participate in it fully. 'It is a great mistake', wrote Archbishop William Temple, 'to suppose that God is interested only, or even primarily, in religion.

What did I learn from the life of Paul Tournier:

I learned four things from Paul Tournier. First, God is interested in every aspect of our life.

Then, if we trust in his guidance, he will lead us in the right way.

Third, if we trust in him completely then whatever task he gives us to do in life will be done in his strength.

Four, we do not all have to be pastors or ministers of the gospel. God is interested in whatever tasks we set ourselves. He will bless our work because no matter what our profession, if we do it in his strength, we are completing his will.

CHAPTER FIFTEEN: MORE WISDOM FROM HISTORY

Wisdom is the ability to use knowledge so as to meet successfully the emergencies of life. Men may acquire knowledge, but wisdom is a gift direct from God (Bob Jones Snr).[85]

MARY SLESSOR (1848-1915).

Are you interested in mission work? Here is the story of a great missionary woman who was honoured by the British government.

It is fascinating to note Mary's background and how her character was formed. Born in Scotland, she learned to look after herself in a rough neighbourhood. Working hard in the local cotton mill and studying hard in her spare time, she showed great strength of will in her determination to be a missionary.

Mary was born second of a poor family of seven children. She grew up hearing stories of missionaries and wanted to follow her two brothers onto the mission field. However, when they both died of pneumonia, she decided she would go instead.

Her father was a shoemaker by trade, but he was an alcoholic and unable to keep his job. Her mother was a deeply religious woman, a skilled weaver who went to work in the mills to support the family. When she was old enough Mary also worked half time at the mill but kept studying half time at school.

She dreamed of Africa, and her favourite game was to teach an imaginary school of black children. She read avidly and was a constant student of the Bible and of Milton's *Paradise Lost*. She began to teach Sunday School to children in her area.

---

[85] Bob Jones Snr. (1883-1968) was an American evangelist, pioneer religious broadcaster, and the founder and first president of Bob Jones University.

A skilled worker

By the age of fourteen Mary was a skilled jute worker, working 12 hours a day. She worked in this factory for 14 years. Her work brought her constantly in contact with the roughest element of the city, but she was able to hold her own against the bullies. She was a marvellous example to the young people of her day and her life and what she accomplished can still be an inspiration to individuals today.

Her mother, a quiet, sweet Christian woman, was a prayer warrior and very interested in a magazine, *The Missionary Record*, published by the United Presbyterian Church. This magazine informed their members of missionary activities and needs.

When Mary learned from this magazine that David Livingstone, the famous missionary explorer had died, she decided to become a missionary to Africa.

Accepted as a missionary

At the age of 28 she was accepted as a Scottish Presbyterian missionary. When she arrived in West Africa, she was assigned to the Calabar region in the land of the Efik people. Here she learned Efik, one of the local languages and began teaching the natives.

Mary had red hair which she kept cut short and blue eyes. She was full of enthusiasm for her new life. On the mission field she became engaged to be married to one of the other missionaries but unfortunately, he took sick and had to return to England where he died. They had to say goodbye to one another knowing they might never see each other again on this earth. What a dedicated couple!

The Calabar region

Mary wanted to go deeper into the Calabar region but contracted Malaria and had to return to England to recuperate. When she returned to the mission field, she was posted to another compound three miles further into Calabar closer to the Efik people. She began to eat the native diet because she wanted to send some of her wages home to her mother and the imported English food was very expensive.

When an inspection was held of the Mission in 1881-82 the deputies were impressed by the work she had done. She was able to accomplish so much because she had learned the Efik language well and ate the same food as the natives. Because of these two things she enjoyed their unreserved friendship and confidence.

After sixteen years on the mission field Mary returned to Scotland to nurse her mother and sister. While there she spent three years speaking at many churches sharing stories of her work in Calabar.

On her return to Africa, she moved yet further away from Central Calabar, from the areas that were already freed from heathen practices.

The native people thought twins were evil

Because the African natives thought twins were evil, they would send mother and babies into the forest to die. Mary began collecting the mothers and their twins and caring for them. She would take the mothers and their babies into her home. She had an ingenious method of rocking the babies to sleep. She had ropes set up with baby hammocks attached. In the night when a baby cried all she had to do was pull on the rope and the hammocks would begin to swing and put the babies back to sleep. In time she convinced the natives that the twins were normal children, and they stopped the practice of leaving them to die in the forest. She saved hundreds of twins who had been left to starve or be eaten by animals.

She also helped with the healing of those natives who were sick and stopped the practice of determining guilt by making the suspects drink poison.

During this third mission she heard her mother and sister had died and this made her more determined to keep going through her sadness, leaning on the Lord for comfort.

Honoured by the British Government

Mary was also the force behind establishing the Hope Waddell Training Institute in Calabar which provided vocational schooling to the Efik people, and she was honoured by the British Government which made her their representative in the Calabar as a Consular Agent.

She was certainly a woman to look up to and admire for her dedication, strong will and determination to do her very best for God. An excellent role model for young women today. Here are some of her famous quotes.[86]

1. Christ sent me to preach the gospel and he will look after the results.

2. Why should I fear? I am on a Royal Mission. I am in the service of the King of kings.

3. My life is one long daily, hourly record of answered prayer. For physical health, for mental overstrain, for guidance given marvellously, for errors and dangers averted, for enmity to the Gospel subdued, for food provided at the exact hour needed, for everything that goes to make up life and my poor service. I can testify, with a full and often wonder-stricken awe, that I believe God answers prayer.

4. If you are ever inclined to pray for a missionary, do it at once, wherever you are.

5. In Christ, we become new creatures. His life becomes ours. Take that word 'life' and turn it over and over and press it and try to measure it and see what it will yield.

---

[86] www.dictionarybook.org/quotes/mary-slessor.html

6. Eternal life is a magnificent idea which comprises everything the heart can yearn after. Do not your hearts yearn for this life, this blessed and eternal life, which the Son of God so freely offers?

7. Prayer is the greatest power God has put into our hands for service, praying is harder than doing, at least I find it so, but the dynamic lies that way to advance the Kingdom.

What did I learn from the life of Mary Slessor?

Mary's life story is an inspiration to serve God with all your heart, soul, mind and strength. She was patient and waited God's timing and she prepared herself for the task ahead of her. We will do well if we copy her patience and her diligence in preparing ourselves for any future task.

THE WILLIAM BOOTH FAMILY[87]

The remarkable association of the Salvation Army was begun by an outstanding couple and the history of their family unit and how they spread the movement world-wide with the help of their sons and daughters makes fascinating reading.

William Booth (1829-1912). Converted in a little Methodist chapel, William became interested in mission work and evangelistic preaching. In 1861 he and his wife became weary of controversy in the Methodist church, so they withdrew and began evangelistic work. This work, first named *East London Christian Revival Society* became *The Salvation Army* by 1878.

William lived to see his organization spread to 55 different countries as he continued to major in missions to the poor, preaching and conducting personal evangelism. He travelled 5 million miles in his lifetime and preached 60,000 sermons. In 1890 he published his

---

[87] A Dictionary of Women in Church History by Mary L. Hammack Pub. By Moody Press Chicago 1984.

great book, *In Darkest England and The Way Out.* In his book he proposed a number of social reforms to improve the living conditions of the poor in Victorian England. He envisioned certain helpful colonies to assist the poor, but the main thrust of his ministry remained to evangelise as he felt Christianity was the answer to life's problems. Here is a famous quote from William Booth which should send an important message to Christians today.

> "There is a day coming when there will be a religion without repentance, a salvation without the Holy Ghost, a Heaven without Hell."

Catherine Mumford Booth was the wife of William booth. She and her husband had eight children, but she found time to preach the gospel and share in the formation of the Salvation Army along with her husband. I do not doubt she had many helpers to give her the time to work alongside her husband and write her books, despite her large family. Her important writings included *The Salvation Army in Relation to the Church and State; Godliness; Practical Religion; Aggressive Christianity and Popular Christianity.*

Here is a quote from Catherine Booth:-

> "Many do not recognize the fact as they ought, that Satan has got men fast asleep in sin and that it is his great device to keep them so. He does not care what we do if he can do that. We may sing songs about the sweet by and by, preach sermons and say prayers until doomsday, and he will never concern himself about us, if we don't wake anybody up. But if we awake the sleeping sinner, he will gnash on us with his teeth. This is our work - to wake people up."

Bramwell Booth, the first son of William and Catherine Booth, succeeded in the leadership of the Salvation Army after his father's death. Trained like Joshua in the presence of Moses he was able to take the reins without any trouble and carry the work on successfully. His wife Florence was a great help to him. They had five children, so she also needed domestic help as she worked outside the home helping prostitutes to begin a new life. At that time girls as young as thirteen were selling themselves or being sold for money so Florence and her husband Bramwell set up homes for pregnant girls and had them taught a trade to free them from prostitution. Florence organised and led the Women's Social Service Network (1882- 1912). She also inaugurated the Home League which introduced women of the slums to simple but efficient methods of home making and child-care. She served as Justice of the Peace for the London district and as one of the visiting justices for prisons for the County of London. Two of her books are *Mothers and the Empires* and *Friendship with Jesus.*

Here is a quote from Florence Booth:-

> "(This is) the Gospel that represents Jesus Christ, not as a system of truth to be received into the mind like I should receive a system of philosophy, or astronomy, but it represents Him as a real, living, mighty Saviour, able to save me now."

Ballington Booth, the second son of General William Booth was also trained by his father for the work of the Salvation Army. He was Commander of the Salvation Army in Australia (1884-1887). As a teenager Ballington began preaching at Salvation Army open-air meetings, where he would often end by singing and playing his concertina. He became a Colonel in The Salvation Army at the age of 23, when he was positioned as a Training Officer. He was later moved to Australia, followed by the United States and Canada. He and his wife Maud seceded from the mother organisation in 1896 and established the more democratic *Volunteers of America in* USA of which he became the president. He wrote the book, *From Ocean to Ocean.*

In 1940 after her husband's death, Maud succeeded him as national president and commander in chief. She became interested in work in prisons and with released prisoners in the United States. In 1892 she was the first Salvation Army officer to be given the license to perform marriages. After that all women officers had that privilege. Maud and Ballington Booth believed in reform and redemption, and those core values led to their *Look Up and Hope* program. Its goal was to break the cycle of poverty for children affected by one or both of their parents being in prison and help them reach their full potential through education. This programme is still going on today. Maud wrote *Branded, Look Up and Hope, After Prison–What? and Twilight Fairy Tales.*

Catherine Booth-Clibborn was the first daughter born to William and Catherine Booth. She married Arthur Sidney Clibborn who then changed his name to Booth-Clibborn. They served the Salvation Army in France but after 21 years they broke away. Catherine was a pioneer in opening France and Switzerland to the Salvation Army. She was much loved, and her preaching reached many lives for Christ. After becoming Pentecostals in 1906 Catherine and her husband continued preaching and spreading the gospel as travelling evangelists in Europe, the United States and Australia. They continued holding crusades for the rest of their lives.

Emma Moss Booth-Tucker was the second daughter and fourth child of William and Catherine. Converted at a young age she spoke in public at just nineteen years of age. She was a leader, writer and hymnist and by the age of twenty was much involved with the Salvation Army. When she married Frederick St. George de Lautour Tucker, he changed his surname to Booth-Tucker. She became director of the first Salvation Army Training College for women and held influential positions in the United States and India where she worked with her husband who held a Commander post there. She was friend to some of the most prominent statesmen and women leaders of the world. Unfortunately, she was killed in a train derailment in Dean Lake Missouri when her eldest child was just thirteen.

Evangeline Cory Booth was the fourth daughter and the seventh child of Catherine and William, and she served the Army well. Evangeline did not marry but served the Lord faithfully, accomplishing great things for God. She led the Salvation Army as Territorial Commander in Newfoundland and Canada and then she led within the United States (1904-1934). Her evangelistic work was demonstrated in the practical application of her faith to relieve suffering and need around the world. She exerted worldwide influence as General of the Salvation Army (1934-1939). In emergencies, earthquakes, flood, fire, famines, and war, she acted quickly sending help to those in need. She must have been a very gifted administrator.

Here is a delightful story told about Evangeline, of the time when gold was first discovered in Alaska and hordes of greedy men rushed to the Yukon to get their share.

> "Evangeline Booth knew the Salvation Army would be needed there. So, she headed north with half a dozen assistants, and arrived to find conditions even worse than she had expected. Vice and lawlessness were the order of the day. Men were shot down for a handful of gold dust, or for no reason at all. Five men were killed the day Evangeline Booth arrived. There were shortages of everything – blankets, food, equipment, clothing – men were quick tempered and surly, and in no mood for sermons. But Evangeline Booth knew what to do. That evening she and her little band stood on the banks of the Yukon River and sang *"Nearer My God To Thee,"* and lonely men began to gather by the hundreds – by the thousands – until nearly twenty-five thousand were lustily singing the hymn! There was singing every day after that...and much less disorder, many less shootings."[88]

Evangeline was honoured with The Distinguished Service Medal, bestowed on her by President Woodrow Wilson, honorary degrees from Columbia University and Tufts College, The Fairfax Gold

---

[88] *Light from Many Lamps,* edited by Lillian Eichler Watson. Pg. 48

Medal for "eminent patriotic services" and the Vasa Gold Medal from the king of Sweden among other distinctions. As a musician she was a harpist, wrote hymns, and composed music for a number of Salvation Army hymns. These are included in her book *Songs of the Evangel* published in 1927. Her other books include, *Love is All, Toward a Better World* and *Women*. The following quote from her shows her philosophy of service to everyone needing help.

> "There is no reward equal to that of doing the most good, to the most people in the most need".

William and Catherine Booth had eight children altogether and five of them served with distinction. Their third daughter, Marian Billups Booth suffered from ill health so was unable to serve in the Army with her siblings. One supposes that similar concerns kept the other two of the eight siblings from serving. However, what a marvellous family they were and what a great amount they achieved for the Kingdom of God through the Salvation Army. Unusual in the Victorian era, all of William and Catherine Booth's children survived into adulthood.

What did I learn from the Booth family?

What a wonderful family the Booths were and how amazing was the prophecy from William Booth that one day there would be a religion without repentance, a salvation without the Holy Ghost and a heaven without hell. We see this in our modern world where there is a lack of repentance and a disbelief in God and a coming judgment. The world without belief in God will descend into chaos. We Christians are praying and believing that God will intervene in our generation. We know he is in control, and we have been promised that when the enemy comes in like a flood the Lord will lift up a standard against him (Isaiah 59:19 KJV).

What if the Booths had decided, like many modern couples, to have only one or two children? What a deprivation for the kingdom of God that would have been. Elon Musk, this world's first trillionaire and an extremely clever man, has warned us if couples do not have larger families, we may soon see the end of humanity.

The genocide of abortion

Already in Japan there are more diapers sold for the elderly than for babies. Unless this turns around the Japanese race will finally fade away into history. Italy and Germany are also in trouble and have welcomed thousands of refugees into their lands to make up the lack of workers. According to the World Health Organisation 73 million babies are aborted each year which amounts to gradual, purposeful, self-imposed genocide. By 2030 there may not be enough young people working to support all the elderly.[89]

The future of humanity

As one of those who have reached an advanced age I am concerned as to the future of humanity. I feel for my grandchildren and my great grandchildren. I wonder what they will face in future years.

For myself I trust in God who is the ultimate victor and know that he has everything planned. However, the Apostle John received a Revelation from God as to the future of mankind on the island of Patmos and his prophecy is overwhelming. War, famine, pestilence, and God's judgment are to come into our world. How long before these things come upon us, we are not told. All we can do is trust that God will work everything out in his good time.

When will Jesus Christ return? As I write the world seems to be in turmoil and atomic war is becoming more and more possible. Russia is attacking the Ukraine, and people are suffering and dying there. We hear of other wars and rumours of wars in the Middle East. The USA is being overwhelmed with aliens from other countries and drugs are pouring over their southern border. Human trafficking has grown, and little children are being stolen and sold for money.

---

[89] Abortion rates by Country 2022, World Population Review

We have already suffered one pandemic with Covid 19 and altogether our world is in turmoil. We need a strong negotiator, someone able to bring honesty, common sense and compassion to the bargaining table to fix the mess we are in. Christians yearn for the second coming of Christ as Jesus seems to be the only one who can bring peace to our troubled world.

> "In fact, a study of the history of Israel and of the church shows that in every time of deep crisis, especially when an existing order is collapsing and the future is dark with uncertainty, people have commonly reacted by yearning for God to intervene and to establish his promised Paradise on earth."[90]

For myself and my dear husband I feel we have lived through the best of times, and we will be long gone before any evil comes upon the earth. For my extended family I must trust in the goodness of God to bring them through to the heavenly kingdom where we will live in eternity with the Lord.

Here are my last words of wisdom to leave with you!

GOD SHOULD COME FIRST

The fool says in his heart, "There is no God" (Psalm 14:1a).

I trust you will not be foolish enough to leave God out of your life. I believe throughout the years to come you will be given opportunities to acknowledge and accept God's love if you haven't already. I trust that you will accept his invitation.

The simplest explanation of the reason God wants us all to accept Jesus Christ as Saviour is included here to help you understand God's reasons for sending Jesus to die on the cross for you and for all mankind:

---

[90] *When the Trumpet Sounds* by Ken Chant Vision Publishing Ramona California 2013. Pg. 101

JESUS' DEATH HAD A PURPOSE

First and foremost, God loves us and wants to have fellowship with us.

> *Here I am! I stand at the door and knock. If anyone hears my voice and opens the door, I will come in and eat with that person, and they with me* (Revelation 3:20).

But because he is a Holy God and cannot look upon sin, he cannot have friendship with us unless we are perfect as he is perfect. Jesus told us in Matthew:

> *Be perfect, therefore, as your heavenly Father is perfect* (Matthew 5:48).

Not one of us is perfect, and we cannot become perfect except through the blood of Jesus.

> *For all have sinned and come short of the glory of God* (Romans 3:23).

We can never be good enough by our own efforts no matter how hard we try, so God has provided a way for us to be good enough through Jesus our Saviour. He is the connection between us and God, the bridge over which we can cross to the Kingdom of God.

> *For God so loved the world that he gave his one and only Son, that whosoever believes in him shall not perish but have eternal life* (John 3:16).

Once we have accepted Jesus and his sacrifice for us God sees us as forgiven and clothed in his righteousness. Now we can have fellowship and friendship with God, and nothing can separate us from his love.

> *For I am convinced that neither death nor life, neither angels nor demons, neither the present nor the future, nor any powers, neither height nor depth, nor anything else in all creation, will be able to separate us from the love of God that is in Christ Jesus our Lord* (Romans 8: 35-39).

Repent and be baptised

But it is important to know that we must repent of our sin and be baptised for full salvation. We cannot just accept Jesus and continue to live as before. Repentance means a turning away from our sin and beginning a new life.

> *Repent and be baptised every one of you, in the name of Jesus Christ for the forgiveness of your sins. And you will receive the gift of the Holy Spirit* (Acts 2:38).

A relationship with Jesus

Jesus' commands must be studied and obeyed, and we must develop a relationship with him through prayer and Bible study. Now it is our privilege to tell others of God's love for them and to teach them of his ways.

Jesus gave us this commission

> *All authority in heaven and on earth has been given to me. Therefore, go and make disciples of all nations, baptizing them in the name of the Father and of the Son and of the Holy Spirit and teaching them to obey everything I have commanded you. And surely I am with you always, to the very end of the age (Matthew 28:18-20).*

My heartfelt prayer is that those of you that have not accepted Jesus as your Saviour yet will one day give your heart and life to him. After 70 and more years as a Christian, I can heartily recommend the Christian life. The peace and joy I have received and the prayers I have had answered have proved to me that God's love is very real.

ADDENDUM ONE

These are my favourite attributes of God.

He is affectionate.

You, LORD, are forgiving and good, abounding in love to all who call on you (Psalm 86:5).

He is just.

He is the Rock, his works are perfect, and all his ways are just (Deuteronomy 32:4)

He is generous.

For God so loved the world that he gave his one and only Son that whosoever believes in him shall not perish but have eternal life (John 3:16).

He is accepting.

The LORD your God is with you, the Mighty Warrior who saves, he will take great delight in you; in his love he will no longer rebuke you but will rejoice over you with singing. (Zephaniah 3:17).

He communicates.

I sought the LORD, and he answered me; he delivered me from all my fears (Psalm 34:4).

He disciplines.

Endure hardship as discipline; God is treating you as his children. For what children are not disciplined by their father? (Hebrews 12:7).

BIBLIOGRAPHY

Adams, Barbara., *It's Called Survival.*, Pub. Hyde Park Press; 2002.

Beder, Sharon., with Wendy Varney and Richard Gosden., *This Little Kiddy Went to Market - The Corporate Capture of Childhood.*, Pub. Pluto Press, London; 2009.

Benner, David G. and Hill, Peter C., *Baker's Encyclopedia of Psychology and Counselling.*, Pub. Baker Books; 1999.

Bushnell, Horace., (1802-1876) *Christian Nurture.*, Pub. Christian Classics Ethereal Library, Grand Rapids, MI.

Carnegie, Dale., *How to Win friends and Influence People.*, Pub. Simon and Schuster; 1934.

Chant, Ken., *When the Trumpet Sounds.*, Vision Publishing; 2013.

Christian Century The., A quote from Jan 31st 1990.

Cloud, Dr. Henry and Townsend Dr. John., *Boundaries.*, Strand Publishing, Sydney;1996.

Collins, Gary R., *Christian Counselling, A Comprehensive Guide.*, Pub. Thomas Nelson; 2007.

DeKoven, Stan., *Journey to Wholeness.*, Vision Publishing; 2000.

.... *Parenting on Purpose.*, Vision Publishing; 1996.

............*Bible in Counselling The.*, Vision Publishing; 2009.

Dobson., *New Dare to Discipline The.*, Pub. Tyndale House Inc.; 2014.

Franklin, Benjamin., (1706-1790) *Autobiography.*, Create Space Independent Publishers; 2018.

Goodwin, David., editor, *Celebrate Children.*, An unpublished set of notes; 2011.

Hammach, Mary L., *Dictionary of Women in Christian History A.*, Pub. Moody Press; 1984.

Inchley, John., *All About Children.*, Pub. Coverdale House; 1976.

Jeffares, Norman A. & Grey, Martin; Editors., *Dictionary of Quotations.*, Pub. Harper Collins, Glasgow; 1995.

Khayyam, Omar., *Rubaiyat The.*, Translation by Edward Fitzgerald, Pub. Bernard Quaritch; 1859.

Langlang, William., *Piers the Ploughman.*, Penguin Books Reprint, Hammonsworth; 1975.

Lewis, C. S., *Screwtape Letters.*, Pub. Geoffrey Bles; 1941.

............*The Four Loves.*, Pub. Harvest Books; 1971.

Metaxas, Eric., *Is Atheism Dead ?.*, Pub. Salem Books 2021.

Myers, David C., *Psychology.*, Pub. MacMillan; 2006.

Moyer, Elgin S., *Wycliffe Biographical Dictionary of the Church.*, Pub. Moody Press, Chicago.

Plimer, Ian., *Green Murder.*, Pub. Connor Court; 2021.

Livingstone, L. P., *Mary Slessor of Calabar* (1848-1915) Biography of a Christian Woman., Lulu.com; 2018.

Sydney Morning Herald., 11th dec. 2003, Aug 26, 2004.

Tournier, Dr. Paul., *The Adventure of Living.*, Pub. Harper and Row; 1965.

Villard., *Spoiled Rotten, Today's Children and How to Change Them.*, Amazon; 1992.

Watson, Lillian Eichler., *Light From Many Lamps.*, Pub. Simon and Schuster; 1951.

WORDS OF INTEREST

ADHD; 45, 97

Anger; 13, 37, 50, 124

Abortion; 80, 103, 171

Authority; 23, 43, 44, 77, 79, 147, 175

Bible; 15, 20, 58, 61, 62, 64, 175

Bipolar; 45

Books; 7, 18, 30, 32, 34, 58, 59

Character; 13, 31, 58, 59, 87, 88, 160

Child, Children   Too many throughout book for results.

Command; 58, 63, 64, 76, 77, 87, 118, 137, 140, 167, 168

Commandments; 58, 64, 76, 118

Control; 39, 45, 60, 61, 70, 85, 125, 126, 129, 130, 133, 134, 137, 171

Culture; 39, 45, 61, 79, 94, 102, 114, 124, 126

Divorce; 19, 31, 36, 43, 52, 53, 64, 149, 150

Discipline; 40, 50, 51, 53, 55, 63, 87, 88, 148, 177

Dysfunctional; 125, 130, 133

Education; 9, 20, 21, 26, 30, 31, 168

Emancipation; 80, 81

Encouragement; 51, 91, 93, 99

Family, Families; Too many throughout book for results.

Father, Fathers; 9, 39, 49, 50, 53, 147

Feelings; 17, 29, 63, 69, 70, 90, 147

Forgiveness; 43, 47, 63, 94, 95, 175

Foster children; 57, 68, 69

Friendship; 34, 35, 112, 114, 120, 139, 162, 167

Future; 9, 19, 20, 43, 45, 48, 172, 173, 175

Genocide; 171, 172

Goals; 19, 91, 95, 135

Happiness; 9, 11, 20, 34, 45, 49, 66, 88, 110, 119, 150

Health, Healthy; 18, 22, 25, 26, 27, 28, 108, 110, 113, 114, 116, 117, 118, 119, 120, 122, 171

History; 20, 33, 49, 79, 110, 142, 151

Humanism; 43, 44, 49, 57, 102, 117

Humanity; 23, 36, 171, 172

Learn, Learning, Learned; 13, 18, 19, 28, 61, 62, 65, 66, 67, 70, 77, 83, 84, 85, 86, 92, 94, 98, 106, 114, 115, 123, 129, 147, 151, 162

Life, Lives, Living; 17, 20, 21, 22, 28, 39, 42, 43, 57, 58, 61, 64, 67, 68, 69, 71, 72, 77, 79, 81, 82, 93, 135, 139, 140, 141, 151, 152, 161, 164, 173

Life Stories; 19, 40, 47, 53, 59, 67, 71, 73, 87, 97, 120, 121, 127, 128, 129, 130, 131, 132, 137

Love, Loved; 34, 37, 45, 50, 52, 53, 55, 57, 59, 62, 63, 64, 66, 71, 79, 82, 87, 94, 101, 102, 104, 106, 107, 110,112, 115, 125, 135, 136, 138, 140, 141, 142, 144, 148, 150, 174, 175

Manners; 36, 37, 38, 39, 46, 74, 103, 121, 139, 147

Marriage; 7, 11, 36, 39, 40, 41, 42, 102, 103, 104, 106, 116, 130, 135, 136, 137, 138, 139, 140, 144, 149, 168

Mature, Maturity; 9, 19, 36, 51, 52, 55, 62, 74, 86, 106, 107, 118, 119, 127, 132, 145

Me generation; 23, 57, 79, 94, 106

Modern; 20, 26, 32, 33, 44, 49, 63, 124, 137, 141, 171

Mothers; 8, 57, 58, 61, 62, 71, 118, 124, 137, 141, 147, 163

Obedience; 39, 51, 55, 63, 73, 74, 83, 87, 146

Parents, Parenting; Too many throughout book for results.

Play; 11, 21, 49, 55, 57, 60, 70, 103, 104, 112, 115, 116, 117

Potty training; 85, 86

Practice; 75, 103

Pre schools; 75

Problems; 45, 75, 88, 104, 105, 121, 133, 135, 138, 151, 156, 157, 166

Proverbs; 15, 16

Relationships; 7, 29, 42, 83, 91, 95, 99

Security; 52, 67, 71, 72, 107, 140, 150

Self esteem; 93

Selfish, selfishness, unselfish; 23, 47, 78, 88, 101, 103, 106, 145, 156,

Skills; 17, 18, 20, 63, 67, 84, 85, 89, 103

Submission; 104, 105, 138

Success, successful; 9, 16, 19, 31, 41, 53, 60, 64, 69, 84, 103

Tact; 17, 37, 38, 107

Tantrums; 87

Training; 9, 52, 75, 76, 85, 86, 87, 90, 91, 146, 163, 167, 168

Trust; 9, 16, 25, 27, 45, 51, 60, 62, 105, 115, 116, 136, 138, 140, 147, 150, 156, 157, 158, 172, 173

Teenagers; 84, 98, 99, 115, 116, 119, 120, 132

Types; 41, 55, 60, 62, 69, 126

Violence; 14, 23, 37, 149

Wisdom; 7, 9, 12, 13, 15, 16, 17, 38, 51, 57, 64, 108, 112, 114, 124, 142, 147, 151, 160, 173

Women's liberation; 39, 58, 81

Working wife; 144

PEOPLE OF INTEREST

Adams Barbara; 106

Addison, Joseph; 11

ADHD; 45, 97

Amiel, Henri F.; 57

Allen, James; 125

Apostle Paul; 79, 90

Beder, Sharon; 49

Beecher, Henry Ward; 101

Benner, David G.; 147

Bennett, Dr.; 54

Booth, Ballington; 167

Booth, Bramwell; 166

Booth, Catherine Mumford; 166

Booth-Clibborn, Catherine; 168

Booth-Tucker, Emma Moss; 168

Booth, Evangeline Cory; 169

Booth, William; 165

Botton Alain; 43

Bushnell, Horace; 145

Carnegie, Dale; 35

Chant, Ken; 20, 82

Collins, Gary R.; 132

Cullen, Delores; 110

DeKoven, Stan; 9, 89, 126

Eliot, Charles W.; 66

Franklin, Benjamin; 152

Gide, Andre; 151

Goodwin, David; 9,49

Graham, Billy; 16

Graham, Ruth; 143

Grandberg, Lars; 106

Gregg, Michael Carr; 54

Griffin, Paul; 67

Henry, Matthew; 106

Horman, William; 36

Inchley, John; 148

Jones, Bob Snr.; 160

Kierkegaard, Soren; 135

Kirkland, Martha; 19

Kolk, Bessel Van Der; 30

Langland, William; 24

Lewis, C. S.; 24, 31, 147

Longfellow, Henry Wadsworth; 97

McDuff, John Rose; 47

Metaxas, Eric; 32

Meyer, F. B.; 105

Meyer, Steven; 33

Meyers, David G.; 83

Moyer, Elgin S.; 141

Overstreet, H. A.; 36

Phelps, William Lyon; 144

Plimer, Dr.; 22

Pratt, Daron; 49

Prince Derek; 52

Francis Raymond; 26

Seneca, Lucius Annaeus; 88

Slessor, Mary; 160

Stevenson, Robert Louis; 93

Talmud; 83

Thoreau, Henry David; 26

Tournier, Dr. Paul; 156

Turnbull, Ralph G.; 139

Washington, George; 47

Watson, Lillian Eichler; 170

Wilbur, Ray Lyman; 110

www.ingramcontent.com/pod-product-compliance
Lightning Source LLC
Chambersburg PA
CBHW051102160426
43193CB00010B/1287